2005

Weathered Pages: The Poetry Pole

1996–2005

Weathered Pages

The Poetry Pole
1996–2005

Jim Bodeen Terry Martin Dan Peters Rob Prout

Editors

Blue Begonia Press · Yakima, WA · 2005

Weathered Pages: The Poetry Pole edited by Jim Bodeen, Terry Martin, Dan Peters, and Rob Prout.

ISBN: 0-911287-52-3

Blue Begonia Press
225 So 15th Ave
Yakima, WA 98902

Grateful acknowledgment to the Breneman Jaech Foundation for a grant that partially funded publication of this book.

Thanks also to Karen Bodeen, Jane Gutting, Elizabeth Miller, Amy Peters and Jackie Prout.

for the poems lost in the weather

CONTENTS

Invisible Guests: The Poetry Pole And Its Invitation

Terry Martin

Poetry—both reading and writing it—reminds me to slow down, to breathe, to be here, now. And I need reminding.

As woo-woo as it may sound, I felt "called" to the Poetry Pole. I didn't know I needed it, but I did. And there it was, planted on the corner of 15th & Bell, surrounded by roses. Visiting it for the first time, I felt as if I were coming home

The Poetry Pole is a creative act, realized. Like someone in whose presence you blossom into who you were meant to be, the Pole reaches out one great arm and holds you kindly. An altar, it helps you acknowledge and reclaim your true size.

It's no accident that the Poetry Pole is planted in a garden. Reading the pages posted there among trees and flowers, I experience the connection to the earth, and to humanity, that is my birthright. Hidden birds sing small songs there.

Writing, especially writing poetry, one works solo and in relative obscurity, for the most part. Posting my poems on the pole, and reading others peoples' work there, reminds me that I'm not the only one engaged in this strange enterprise. Others, too, foster time for quiet contemplation and inner work, make their lives hospitable for the muse, leaving ample room for surprise, mystery, delight—yielding to, not opposing the flow. A restlessness enters and grows, the slightest leaning starts, a tilting toward the next thing, and we begin.

The Poetry Pole is a living reminder that I'm not alone. Inviting a shift from isolation to connection (what the narrator of *The*

Grapes of Wrath describes as moving from 'I' to 'we'), it's about belonging: the longing of my being and the being of my longing.

Some days I drive by and stop to read the pages pinned to the wood. White flags, waving surrender to the muse. Tell-tales, signifying which way the wind is blowing. Some are weathered—rain, like tears, blurring words and edges.

Offerings include inventive, brave, quirky, politically alert, funny, heartbreaking poems. Dreams, musings, edgings toward truth. Happy accidents, the 'not logic' gifts. Broken places. Inadequacies, terrible and abundant. The blank spaces. The range of the work posted on the pole arrests with surprises: tentative first efforts to express personal truths, brilliant originality, deep, somber unforgetting. Room there for works-in-progress, too, which each of us is, after all.

The strength of the Poetry Pole is its resistance to formula.

On those pages, flapping in the wind, individuality and diversity are givens. Reading the work posted there is a reminder of what, ultimately, unites those of us who write: not region, not color, not belief, but loving language and honoring imagination. In these divided times, the search for common experience becomes even more necessary.

> "The purpose of poetry is to remind us
> how difficult it is to remain just one person,
> for our house is open, there are no keys in the doors,
> and invisible guests come in and out at will."
>
> Czeslaw Milosz
> "Ars Poetica"

Invisible guests coming *in and out at will*. Yes. Like poetry, the Poetry Pole reminds me that there is no separation, really, between us. How easily I can forget that.

Faith in ourselves and each other in this world, is a job. Denied certainty, we engage with what comes, with what arrives. And the medicine we need is always arriving, and moving in next door to us. For me, the Poetry Pole is medicine. An *open house…no keys in the doors*, it addresses our deeply human desire to tell the truth to ourselves and to each other, providing us with the means of our own redemption.

It's hard to explain why I find posting one of my poems there to be every bit as satisfying as receiving a "yes" letter in the mail, signifying acceptance in a national literary journal or magazine. One reason may be that for me, submitting work for publication requires stepping carefully between ego landmines, like ambition, competition, and envy. Arrogance and inferiority, too—those twin traps.

The Poetry Pole has nothing to do with striving. The same energy that impels me to write poems impels me to carry them to the Pole.

Another reason is surely the "addressable thou" at the other end; I know my most recent effort will be read by Jim Bodeen, the Keeper of the Pole, with care, and by interested others, too. Pinning my page to the wood is one way of making contact. That's what I want, what I need, at core.

Ironically, I find the impermanence of the act of posting my work on the pole to be oddly satisfying, too. What I didn't know along the way was that this work would be gathered, saved, re-read, preserved, and ultimately shared with a wider audience, in the form of this text. "I came into this world to live out loud," Emile Zola wrote. The Poetry Pole is one way those of us represented in this book do that. I wish to express my gratitude for the pleasure of being in their company.

TENDING THE POLE

Rob Prout

THE NEEDLE IN THE GARDEN

Dan Peters

Eight years ago, in 1997, I put a poem on the Poetry Pole and it changed my life.

But before I tell my story, I'd like to explain how I've come to see the Poetry Pole. The pole, with the word POETRY carved on the east and west sides, sits one block from the political boundary of east and west Yakima. It's one block from the line between north and south Yakima. It is the fixed point between my home in Selah and my job as a teacher at Yakima Valley Community College. It lies between my work and my wife's job at the hospital. It is a ten-minute walk from my classroom, making it a perfect field trip for YVCC's creative writers who want to put their work up where people can see it. Whenever we take that walk, I hope they think about what they have done on the way back to school. When they post on the pole, they have read their poem into the record. They have recorded their story for the community to see and hear. Pinning a poem to the pole is a way to bear witness. It is a way to testify.

The pole is an unpredictable journal. There are submissions, but no editor. There are no regular publication dates. In fact, there are long stretches when it is as bare as a tree in January, and its silence can feel like winter and make you doubt. Other times you see from a distance white sheets moving in the breeze like prayer flags but can't stop and look, and when you go back, the poems are gone. It is the stump that performers rub for luck before they go on at the Apollo Theater. It is a literary trellis, around which things wind, grow, climb and bloom. The pole is practical and beautiful. It is sweet and useful.

The pole is the needle on the record.

It is also the threaded needle. If *story* comes from *suture*, through Sanskrit for *thread*, the Poetry Pole is the needle that stitches our stories together. The pole has something for you. Something that makes you want to meet the writer. Something that, standing there amid the flowers or the snow on Bell Avenue, makes you want to speak. Something that, like a stitch, closes a gap, makes a connection. The pole is generous this way.

That's where my story about the Poetry Pole comes in.

When I was a senior in high school, in the fall of 1986, I was involved in a fatal accident. I was the driver and a small boy died. His name was Roberto. For ten years, I fought with the consequences of that late summer afternoon. In the *Afterword*, Jim talks about being called to poetry. I think that's why we are friends. Without trying to balance the equation, or provide a reason for the accident, I think that's what happened to me. I was called.

Ten years after the accident, I went on a long car trip with a friend from college who did not know about accident. Because we were friends, I tried to find a way to talk to him about it. I couldn't do it. It had been a secret for so long that I didn't have any words for it.

When I returned home, I started to write about the journey. Like the attempts to talk to my friend, my first efforts to explain were not up to the job. I wrote a short poem about walking through a tunnel on a hike. I thought it captured what I wanted to say about the accident. I showed the poem to a friend. We talked about it briefly but I could tell that all the heavy metaphor and symbolism I'd worked into the poem had been rightly missed. In fact, after talking to my friend I realized there was nothing in the poem about the accident. Because I identified so strongly with the event, I assumed others saw the grief and doubt on my face every day.

But people don't see through us so easily. That's the way poems are sometimes when you don't show them around. Your metaphors become too private. Most of the time you can put it aside and write the next one. For me, that didn't seem possible. Out of respect for what had happened, for the loss, I wanted to tell the story right.

I went back to the start of the road trip, which eventually led me back to the day of the accident. I worked on the poem section by section for a year. I finished the poem in early August, almost eleven years after the initiating event. I printed off the 13 pages I had written and read them to my wife, Amy. I got in the car and drove to the Poetry Pole.

I think the idea of putting the poem on the pole came to me that day. I wanted the secret out of my house. It was a risk that was important to the meaning of the poem. Right then, it was the only thing to do.

If I didn't write for the Poetry Pole then, I do now. When you write with the Poetry Pole in mind, the imagined audience changes. There is much to be said for writing for yourself alone. And there is a value in writing for an audience that is known, for your family or friends. But when you post on the pole, the relationship between the reader and the writer is less certain. Although it is customary to sign your work, passersby likely won't know who you are. Often, the reader and the writer are unknown to each other. This anonymity causes you to reconsider your metaphors. The Poetry Pole keeps you from living too much in your own head, from believing you are transparent.

What I do remember, clearly, is the moment I put the poem on the pole. It was hot. The Bodeens' garden was dry. The flowers around the pole were blooming, but brown on the edges. It was grasshopper weather. I got out of the car with the poem and stuck it to the pole with a push-pin. I remember that part very clearly, forcing the pin through all the pages. I didn't feel brave. I didn't expect anything. Like Terry Martin says, that's not why you put the poems on the pole. You put them there for the town you live in. You put them there to encourage others to speak. You put them on the pole because you have a responsibility to tell your story. It isn't the end of your responsibilities, but the people who post believe that the health of a town depends on storytelling.

After I pinned the poem up, I stood back and looked at it. It looked good there in the middle of all those flowers. It looked like a memorial. I hadn't expected that. I got in my car and drove home. The story about the accident was part of the record. I felt OK.

Then Jim called. He told me the poem would be with me for a long time. I wasn't sure what he meant, but it was not how I saw it. It was on the pole now and out of my control.

In hindsight, the pole was a good place to articulate what I learned from the accident. Poems on the pole, like us, like grief, have a life. The pole is natural. Inclusive. The pole is a four-by-four cedar koan. It is silent and a place for music. It's impermanent. It is always there. You can't predict what will come next. New stories go up and are taken down, but they don't go away. It is random enough to be like everything that is found in the deepest parts of us. Like the town we live in, the Poetry Pole is unpretentious, humble and universal.

It turns out, Jim was right about the life of my poem about the accident. Many things have happened to the poem since then. The poem was turned into a chapbook that was published the same weekend I started teaching at West Valley High School in Yakima. A month after I started teaching, a month after my thirtieth birthday, a month after the chapbook came out, a month after the eleventh anniversary of the accident, I arrived at work one morning and found a prepared statement from the principal on my desk that I read to my first period class. A student at the high school had been involved in a fatal car accident involving a student at an elementary school.

Because of the Poetry Pole and the chapbook, the guidance counselor knew about my story and after a few weeks, sent the student to talk to me. I wasn't the student's teacher and didn't know him very well, so our conversation was brief. At the end of our talk, I gave him the chapbook. If it never did anything else, the Poetry Pole helped that happen.

Three years after the chapbook, Jim called again and asked if I was interested in working on putting the long poem together with other poems for a new collection. Strange things happened along the way to the book's publication—the first run was in a train wreck, which I learned about on the twelfth anniversary of the accident—but when it arrived in Yakima we set up a reading. For the first half hour I read poems from the later sections of the book. Finally, I read from the long poem about the accident.

After the reading, I talked with friends and family. I was relieved that it was over. After signing a book, I looked up and saw two women I did not know, a mother and daughter, standing in front of me. I asked how they would like me to sign the book and the woman said, "I am Roberto's mother."

With her daughter translating, she said, "I pray for Roberto, and I pray for you, too." There are many ways to interpret this statement, but I've come to believe our meeting was a gift. A long sought connection was made. A gap was closed. I believe the Poetry Pole, the needle in the garden, was at work.

There have been other chance meetings brought about by the Poetry Pole. Some of them have been recorded on the corner of Bell Avenue. I met Jenifer Lawrence, a poet and engineer from the Olympic Peninsula, at the Centrum Writers' Conference in Port Townsend several years ago. Her story, some of which you will read here, is sewn to mine. Her perspective and response to a childhood accident is a gift to any one who reads it.

And last summer, when the poem about the accident seemed distant to me, I got a long letter from Michael Daley, a poet, publisher and teacher from the Skagit Valley. He lives with an accident, too. Our correspondence was brought about by a conversation started on the pole.

From the accident, to the student at the high school, to Roberto's mother, to Jenifer, to Michael, the line lacing our stories together is bright and unmistakable and would not exist without the randomness and simplicity of the Poetry Pole. And it isn't just me. The Poetry Pole offers our stories to the world. You are holding what the needle in the garden has gathered. As you read the poems in this book, consider what they share. See what you share. Imagine all our stories pinned and flying from a cedar post not quite in the center of town.

WHEN a dream is born in you
With a sudden clamorous pain,
When you know the dream is true
And lovely, with no flaw nor stain,
O then, be careful, or with sudden clutch
You'll hurt the delicate thing you prize so much.

"A Pinch of Salt" by Robert Graves

scent of ov
summer sun and
is words began to rise.

— Emil

A. K.

WOMEN GATHER

in the kitchen celebrating.
"It's the lopped-off breast party,"
your mother says,
as you stuff green snow peas—
green as the purple gladiola's stems
which you picked up
at Albertson's this morning—
3 for $10—
this same morning
that the local paper carried
a story of 2 brothers,
14 or 15, who grew
gladiolas, "glads,"
as your mother's friend calls them,
in their back yard—
trying to make their bank accounts
grow, the scattering seeds, growing
into the boys' futures.

And here these women sit,
sipping chardonnay, celebrating
a questionable future,
their dangling metal jewelry
reflecting the nightlight skipping
off the river below.

One of these women, an anthropologist,
starts picking dirt
from under her fingernails, wiping
it on a white, crocheted doily,
mud from spending days standing

A. K.

in river beds, scooping,
hands digging through silt,
unearthing bones, the oldest
known bones in the Americas—
bones that have been loved—
bones who've spent an eternity
in the all-encompassing embrace
of warm mud from this desert
river. Now dug up,
kept in temperature-controlled
rooms—their future questionable,
Who do the dead truly belong to?
Women gather in the kitchen
surrounded by gladiolas,
celebrating, eating stuffed
snow peas and blanched
asparagus dipped in extra-virgin olive oil.
And these women also eat
gladiola pollen and seed,
scattered over peas and peppers,
accidents from their place
as garnishes on Wedgewood
serving platters.

Women gather in the kitchen,
celebrating lopped-off breasts
while gladiolas take root
in their stomachs, thick
green stalks creeping and growing,
blooming out open lips in words
of joy and celebration.

John Akins

On the Way to Khe Sanh

—azimuth—a horizontal distance
expressed as degrees of a compass reading

We hold up in the Truong Son Mountains.
The point man shoots an azimuth.
The jungle swallows landmarks on the map;
compass readings guide us.
A bend in the trail separates me from other Marines in the column.

My pack under my legs, I sit back against the elephant grass.
I pull salt-caked creases away from my crotch,
from the crooks of my elbows.
I coax a C-ration tin from my pack,
throw away the crackers,
lay the thin, foil-wrapped disk of chocolate on my thigh,
slip my near-empty canteen from my hip.
This is the last of my water.
I hold a sip, then let it seep down my gullet.

My front teeth find the first groove of concentric lines
scored into the chocolate.
I taste cocoa and sweetness,
tongue the buttery texture,
chase tiny bites with a swig of water.
It cuts the burn of straight chocolate.

I lick my lips,
forget how little time I have been in country-
how many day and nights we will grind toward Khe Sanh.
I sink into stillness and water and chocolate.

GOING BACK TO KY AN WITH COLE

I look back at my 16-year old son
bent over a skittering sand crab.
Ahead, the coastline weaves into the horizon.
The beach is deserted,
like it was 34 years ago.
Then, five of us hunted Communist guerillas.
Jungle separated two hamlets,
Ky Phu and Ky An, the hostile one.
Now, there are more small fishing boats
beached above the tide line.
The hamlets are linked by small brick and adobe huts.
It looks like a realtor's street of dreams.
I show my son the high ground—
this looks like the place we dug our bunkers, I say.
We move along.
Here is where Keig and Marcos were killed.
This is where Ooten and Cronin were wounded.
I flew over our area with a spotter pilot—
called in a six-jet air strike.
Mick Jagger played in my headset.
This is where the Vietnamese Goddess of War
lured me to the dark night, I say.
We walk into the interior.
This is definitely where
the beach meets the jungle, Cole says.
We drink shots of rice whiskey
with some 20-year olds.
You know what's so great, I say:
Now, I'm a 56-year old young man
in the same place I turned old at 19.

Carmela Alexander

AGNES & PAT

Exuberant Agnes chose the large rug canvas,
five by eight,
bags of yarn.
For months she toiled in one rose-patterned corner.

Her friend Louis, craft handy, offered help.
Three months later
he called for more yarn.
And again more.
Flora says she swept up lint all winter.

In spring, rug complete, they invited Agnes and Pat
to collect it.
All four laughing,
Agnes promised,
If I go first, Louis, you get the rug.

Pat delivered it this week.
And sat solo,
on the sofa,
one point of a triangle now.

Jody Aliesan

WHERE WE STAND NOW

this bruise-red stone began
as sand in narrow waters
between two rafts of earthen skin
now called europe north america
before the first time they pulled apart

       sand worn off volcanoes
       fused by its own weight
       bumped up in another undulation
       low places made high

this mound the people call
Cruach Mhárthain / *stack of lastingness*
far below us the great glen
folds tombs and walls made of it
back six thousand years

       see that stream cut the glen
       where it falls to the sea
       it drops tumbled boulders
       the high made low again

look under your feet:
this bloodclot stone's cobbled with
pebbles of blue inlaid in their turn
with grains of shell white
three mountain chains gone

       but persistent as instinct
       ancestor memory

Aliesan

former lives in this one life
strata of fate

• • •

no trees here
from mountaintop to seacliff
conquerors felled them all
    for shipyards smelters
    great hall beams barrel staves
    to demoralize the people
    deprive them of refuge

tree ghosts cloud the slopes
their names haunt speech
roadsign memorials
map-page history:

    Derry *doire* oakwood
    Kylemore *coill mór* great forest
    what's left of *Sailléille*
    a stick in the hand

what shall we do for timber?
the last of the woods is down
the singer grieved
probing for bog-preserved pine

    dead four thousand years before
    Coillte's marching conifers
    squared clear-cut curves
    on land too fair for defeat

Aliesan

· · ·

what then of these mountains these stones
we stand on standing between us
dispossessed native invading settler
trading places over time
sharing the same body
aspects of mind

petrified ash powdered shell bone
it will take another continental shift
the next great mountainbuilding
before we are inclusions together
in a handsized beachcobble
ready to be kissed or thrown

Aliesan

Please Post

> His disciples questioned him and said to him, *Do*
> *you want us to fast? How shall we pray? Shall we*
> *give alms? What diet shall we observe?*
>
> Jesus said, *Do not tell lies, and do not do what you hate.*
> —Gnostic Gospel of Thomas

these days we expect to be lied to
every day we figure what governments announce
corporations claim and management demands
is false blown up or incomplete
manufactured to manipulate

we expect two months or twenty years
after wars are over deals completed deadlines met
we'll finally find out what really happened
one thing we know for sure it'll be
different from what we're told right now

but it's all right to lie   we hear
to children sick and dying strangers enemies
if the liar feels superior or scared enough
that includes us all   *reality cannot be known*
the truth is relative   they say

confusing facts with ethics   I may not know
the truth but I've a notion when I'm lied to yes
and I know when I'm lying
to impress control save face preserve my privacy
protect from hurt do harm   so how about you

Aliesan

what everybody knows but no one speaks
the Kiriwina of New Guinea call *mokita*
and a physicist writes that secrecy
conceals failure more often than success
short memories preserve good consciences
philosophers warn us cynicism
does not expose illusion it's another kind
of show but simply to arrive at that awareness
is holding hands with truth

choose rather to be wrong than false

Aliesan

Before You Leave the Country

on a risky mission
give to every beggar on the street
drop three quarters in the bent paper cup
of the young black sidewalk sorcerer
who says check your itinerary
make sure you have enough resources
know the break point when to cut and run
and the safe place to breathe while you can

go where they sell gargoyles
to buy protection and of course
when you ask for the fierce one Michael
there he is hanging on a chaplet
of snowflake obsidian beads nine times three
red-haired Chloë understands when
you can't tell her why you need him
she'll light candles while you're gone

obey your travel agent wear dark clothes
buy the smallest flashlight you can find
quiet shoes with good traction tin of polish
for your face don't worry about credit cards
they won't question the shopkeepers
who can't give away anything anyway
because you don't know yet yourself
what happens in the next act

what you do know
makes your life a performance
don't pack any prop that might cause
the slightest hesitation when
in some open field you have to drop it
and leave it lie in wet grass

Linda Andrews

DOWNWIND

Last night I swam toward you. The water
was black as sleep and I rolled through the swells
toward your shore.

Closing the distance was as simple
as throwing myself in the outgoing tide.
The only lights were the quarter moon,
the phosphorescent outline of my body
and the lamp in your cabin window, a cool
hundred miles downwind.

All signs were favorable: the kelp waving, whales
like soft buoys to mark the channel, night birds
wrapped in speed screaming back at the wind. Soon
gravel underfoot and the heavy climb
back onto the earth.

Sparks were rising from your chimney—you were burning
my roof again. The truckful of old shingles you brought
from my house to yours were still rising through the forest
one by one. With me, the wood was shelter, heavy
and responsible. Here, it's airborne, incandescent
in the crazy science of turning stability to tinder.

I'm washed clean from my long sail. Let us start over,
your green shirt wrapped around me.

Elizabeth Austin

IN PRAISE OF ORALITY
An Infant Manifesto

only love the world wetly
lean in, lick the nearest anything
bathe it in sweet spit, the delicious
suck of discovery

oh mouth, oh omnivorous organ!
oh edible world!

soon, soon we meet by sight
arm's length, in words—
leaving more and more
world untasted

E. B.

SITTING HERE

Sitting here
I look straight forward
to keep from getting in trouble
the pod officer with her blue eyes
staring at everyone in the room
not a person she misses
not a thing she don't catch
her screaming to those who aren't good
heads turning to see who's getting into trouble
a smile on my face because it isn't me
one more reason to keep looking straight
forward.

Dick Bakken

BASHO'S WORKSHOP

Silent beside a pond
the poets sit around big-eyed,
mouths full of tongue.

BLACKFEET

Two maidens laughing
hang from pintos

pulling up wild peas
in the rain.

ORCHARD

Woman, barefoot,
apple in hand.

When she bites
the spoiling fruit

her lips are sweet
and tart.

Bakken

MARGE

She made pickles and hard love
all weekend, then ran off
with forty pounds
of cucumbers in a suitcase.

PRIEST OF THE BEES

O my happy son lifting
his arms in the bee swarm,
bees bearding his face!

RIPE CHERRIES

Sweet flesh! Juice
slides behind the tongue,
dribbles out the lips.

The hearts fill your mouth
till you spit.

Bakken

THE BLACK-RATSNAKE RITUAL
—*for Marge Piercy*

Through her pampered beanyard
comes the well repairman snorting
in his overalls.
—*Be careful of my beans!*
He cuffs spider thread out of his way.
—*Don't hurt them!*
He feels like throwing his tool box—right
down her busted well—at the
four-foot snake hissing in that hole
full of bugs. The woman,
hair shooting out thick, black, jumps out
of her vines. She never lets him spray the bugs.
Because spiders in the well
eat them. The mice eat the spiders. The snake
eats the mice. She dumps beans
out of a paper bag,
glaring at his heavy boots and hammer.
—*I don't want you hurting my snake.*
He tromps around the well bitching to himself,
sidestepping her beans, while she
disappears deep into the hole with his flashlight.
He slaps his overalls
when he hears her wooing and clucking
and rolls his eyes up at the sky.
There's something like a kiss.
Then she's up grinning with the furious snake
round and round in the paper bag.
Down goes the grumbling
repairman. Snorts and scuffs resonate up
through the well.

Bakken

She keeps watch on his flash beam,
on his sniffing and clanking.
He feels her watching, feels bugs all over him,
curses, slams off the light to kick
at dusty gobs of webs.
—*And don't you hurt any of my mice either!*
He sneezes, bumps his head hard.
—*Son of a—*
—*What?* she calls down, wanting to see, nearly
stepping on her beans. —*What?*
Hand on forehead, he blinks up dazed
through the long narrow dark, sees stars and stars . . .
around a black shape, a vine-haired woman
leaning far above, peering
down, holding a big lumpy bag.

Molly Bales

La Dolce Vita

8.28
After David Hille's wedding reception, sitting in a Starbucks
in downtown Spokane:

conflict
pulses through my veins
honesty suppressed under
the veil of protection
eager anticipation
tormented
storms of future regret
shadow the pleasures of now

8.30
Two days later at 6 am I slide a note under his door and walk out of
my house with coffee in hand:

Loss of Focus.
Convicted.
Forgive?
Safe Travels. God Bless. & Goodbye.

8.31
While driving home from work the call comes minutes before breaking:

desired words of forgiveness proceed
congenialities
respect is birthed
focus returns
reaching for the tip of the iceberg
attention to detail
restores freedom in the big picture

Julie Barker

IN THE THIRD DRAWER OF MY DRESSER

Eighteen full slips receive invitations tonight,
a brief appearance before the mirror.
One after another each glides over the head,
silky nylon cascading breathlessly to knees.
Slender straps adjust lacy cups.
Playful minis beg to get out more often,
one, a shower gift in luscious lemon-yellow.
High school, vivid chartreuse
hid under purple poplin
speckled with matching springtime.
Pale sky blue trimmed with delicate beige lace,
sister's Christmas gift attended Daddy's funeral.
Hand-me-down, exquisite queen of all,
white with lace garland and pleated ruffle,
beneath which elegant gown of Mom's did you dance?

Folded, smoothed, bedded down
amidst rolled-up stockings, crew and argyle socks,
excited slips murmur in the dark.
Hush now, lest your whispers arouse
nightgowns dreaming restlessly in the drawer above.

Lee Bassett

AFTER MAKING LOVE

After the frenzy hip-bone music, after our bodies
And our feeling are the same for a moment,
After we found the flower in the flower in the flower,
We lay back in the burnt wordless afternoon,
And our soul floats calmly out the window.

We see a great blue heron stab a blood-frog in half.
We hear a hyena-dog crack the hard bones in his mouth.
We smell a king vulture who sucks the red carrion eyes.
We taste a wasp whose dying sting is a black sour salt.
We touch an old man, swift-grabbing in a garbage can
Looking for food, or for the best item to sell,
Or perhaps he is looking for something beautiful.

NEAR THE END

Near the end, that is when my Mother walks
Into an ancient Chinese painting
And she walks into the fog.

A fisherman is there, with his long black
Boat full of morphine, but we never
See him again.

Near the end, that is when my Mother's pain
Vibrates with a young monk
Watching a ghostly waterfall.

A sunset is there, with swallows flying
And a kingfisher on a dry reed.
And a disjointed song.

Near the end, that is when my Mother's sleeping
Eye-lids are shocked by summer lightning
And we are there to hold her hand

And we are there to hold her scattered light,
The noble light of surprise.

Bassett

UFFIZI I

A young woman's delight and smile,

childlike, wet, and eccentric,
a salvation I stumble upon

in the dry dust of the Tuscan rooms

where multi-layered, and with the same
sly care of the Masters,

another enthralling,

from another dream of another chance
of rekindling, she pulls her top
sweater off, and departs.

Someday the soul and the body
will lie down together, not now.

Jim Bertolino

LET NATURE

Let nature
express,

by your
quirky speech

and hesitant
touch, its

incomprehensible
intellect.

Jim Bodeen

THE GREAT ROUND

My mother hands me a bouquet
of dried flowers and points out
the dried seed pod she calls Silver Dollar.
She shows me how to extract
the seeds and tells me about alternating years
of silver pods and purple blossoms.
She gives me seeds in a white envelope.
I scatter them in the old roses.
She doesn't tell me they'll be everywhere.
I didn't ask and now I'm surrounded
by a money plant I can't get rid of.
I pull an armful of plants from the bed,
thinking of my mother's gift
and the white envelope of seeds.
Arms too full, just as I turn to drop them
in the wheelbarrow, they fall
from my arms onto the path of bark
winding through the roses. I say to myself
cleaning up, I could have asked more questions.
This morning, months later, I kneel on the path
where these plants fell last summer.
Seedlings everywhere.
Hundreds of them dropped by chance.

Bodeen, J

HOUSE FULL OF LOVE

Walk just past your old habits
and turn whichever way you want.
Share a room with someone
who has come farther than you
and still lives in danger.
The church I attend lists the names
of the dead on the walls where
its members praise God. I drink
from the common cup. I listen
to people who live without evidence
of promise. What is worth
taking with us? Think for a minute
what it must be like for the undocumented.
Now name yourself. Because that's
just who you are. You belong
to the spiritually undocumented.
One day you'll begin to get the idea.

Bodeen, J

BEGINNING AGAIN

This could be how stories saved my life.
Stories and the landscape of faces
before the camera, thrill me.
When people give me their stories,
I try and line up their words on the side.
Simple things—where they were born,
and when. *Where are your grandparents
buried?* I've been given one word:
Storypath/Cuentocamino.
And the command to find out.
That's all I have. Earlier this summer,
a friend visited the burial site of Robert Graves.
I'm listening to him again,
and studying Spanish.
My house feels like a hotel
except for my clothes to pick up.
Clothes themselves are ghosts
of a former self. My wife gets up
and goes to work, kisses me goodbye.
I'm here with the dogs. We do ok.
I strap myself into this chair asking,
What does she look like, this Goddess?
In whose voice will I find her song?

Karen Bodeen

MERRY CHRISTMAS

My gift of love comes from my sewing and not from words.
Now it is time for words.
I love you and appreciate you for all you do for the family,
in talking from your heart and sharing your love
with each one of us. You are never quiet
about sharing and giving to your family.
Your spirit lives in our children and
is appreciated by all.

I'm too quick to be critical and not quick enough to praise.
You are always quick to praise. I love you for your praise.
I have learned much from you but
I'm hoping I still have time to learn more.
I am a slow learner in that way.
I don't have much experience with apology.

Thank you for your energy, spirit, praise and love.
You continue to be my teacher.
I have loved you for thirty-three years.
I will continue to love you for life.

Love, Karen

Your wife and partner
December 26, 1998

Linda Clein Brown

CHICKEN FRICASSEE

It took forty years to forgive my mother
her chicken fricassee. Each week
she filled a pot with chicken parts:
wing tips and backs, gizzards and necks,
bony extrusions unsuited to childish needs.

Mother ruled a watery graveyard,
stirring Hecate's caldron, singing and stirring.
Carcasses of despair swam in her iron kettle
on those disparaging December nights.
Summoned by the moment, we had to confront
an offering of such paltry remnants, bowls
heaping with broth so fowl, so foul. How could
a mother's love be so thin and parsimonious?

The years bring redemption, magical gifts:
memories of those wintry times,
a small kitchen, steam rising
from a murky sea of tiny flagships
and reedy whistles. Silvered windows
like slivers of mercury where a child
sucks on hard shards of flutes, bony treasures,
savoring the rich sound of a mother's song.

Lindsay Brown

What We Don't Know

There are two corners,
on Interstate 90, near Snoqualmie Pass
that scare me almost as much as this.
I drive back to Yakima today,
on solid ground, still not knowing.
I know these roads, though.
I know these mile markers and exit numbers.
These roads know me.
The snow is starting to melt in the mountains
and I am starting to hate this back and forth.
This Seattle to Yakima.
This Yakima to Seattle.
I have been doing this back and forth
for one year and five months now
and I don't know if I will ever stop
or stand still or choose a city.
This interstate is all I have.
I am spilling out, on to these roads.
I say these lines out loud, memorizing them.
I say them all the way to Roslyn.
I say them over and over again—
past Cle Elum, into Ellensburg and
all the way into the valley.
I say them on the way up the stairs.

This morning, in the living room that I left
one year and five months ago,
I drink coffee with my parents.
I drink out of the yellow mug,
the one with the small crack
that runs all the way down the side of it.

Brown, L

My coffee is the color of my skin this morning—
almost exactly.
I blow into the cup, cooling it down,
making ripples that are plain and pure and steady.
My mom asks when I am coming home
and I break down
and I tell her about the hills in Yakima
and how they hold that city together
and how Yakima has held me together.
I tell her how the city looks from the
back fire escape on balmy August nights.
I tell her that I don't really know anything,
that I am unable and unstable
and no, I don't know when I am coming home.
All I really know are these roads, and
these bends and breaks.
And these corners.
I know that I will not uproot—not yet.
I will do this back and forth and
I will drive past these corners
and I will be scared
and I will keep up this routine,
on this interstate.
I will drive through these mountain passes and
watch these seasons fade into each other.

Today, in Yakima
the snow is starting to melt in those hills
and for the first time since last September
I open the window in the kitchen
and I breathe in sweet sharp spring air.
I take in this new season
and this is all I need to know, now.

Bonnie Buckley

HOUSE MUSIC

As much with my foot as my ears
My bare foot rests
Sounds come to me
Buzzes, crackling and rattling
Inconsistent
Distracted
Bring a serenade
The wedding was pure spirit
Sacred space
Extemporaneous speech
Pine boughs and white lights
Alive in her belly, a silent participant
Cold mountain sends cool air
Trees gather spiked along the slopes
Alternately weeping and swooning
He must go out to forage and hunt for food
Finally, he dies of exposure
Waking from a dream
I dream again
Cold from the air
Skyscape decorates the air with water
All of us adventurers, travelers in space and time
This house holding abundant laughter and song
Spilling through the floors and windows
Guitar and violin and voices
Three contemporary Mexicans
Soundscape for a space
Keep to the path

"...a glance that grows blind from ~~~~
and sees blind,
a fire that is wild to go out,
a peace that wakes up storms,
a storm that brings peace...

Ciril Zlobec, "Almost a Hymn"

Anne Byerrum

BROTHERS AND SISTERS

I see the mark on the closet wall
that recorded the date of my cousin's death,
the first death to take my breath away.
Oriena was a cousin who was a sister.
Born from my mother's twin.
I needed to record the pain somewhere,
where only I would know it was there.
The closet was my answer.

This closet has returned in a dream
to be remodeled to fit my new clothes,
a place I can easily gather what I need,
a hidden space between two rooms,
never before explored.
It would mean making changes,
tearing out and putting back
the pain marked in ink.

Now my brother, Jerry, calls.
Oriena's brother, Johnny has died.

In the early years of my life
I had cousins, Oriena, Johnny and Dennis;
all born from my mother's twin.
They lived upstairs across the street
with a large green lawn between us.

Oriena was older in years and
as my mind grew and expanded
hers stayed the same till she died
just after I turned sixteen on a sunny day in May.

Byerrum, A

On my day, I held her hand to come see
the irises outside the bedroom window.
I told her they bloomed just for my birthday,
This year was the first time she did not play
the annual game with me.

Now her brother, my brother/cousin is gone.

I was older than Johnny by two weeks.
We met every day on the grass lawn
playing hide and seek,
bathing in large tin tubs, and
picking lilac leaves for play money.

I went out into the world and moved far away.
Johnny stayed in his home to heal his parents
wounded by Oriena's death.

I would share my life and Johnny would ask
Was I happy? Was this who I loved?
How were my children? Was I doing what I wanted?

He told me he was happy. He walked every day to
buy fresh food for the day's meals. Greeted the neighbors,
treated my aunt with good food and loving company.
And he would ask again, Was I happy? Was I doing what I wanted?

My sister, Avis, and I wrote to Johnny before he died.
Denny found his brother gone and the letters on the table.
Reading the letters he would have known
our children were well and we were happy
and doing what we wanted.

Byerrum, A

Tonight, my brother, George, and I talk to Denny.
I hear our voices over the phone
layering each other's sentences with memories.
We know so much is the same but different since
we played on that large green lawn and
I marked the closet wall.

Sev Byerrum

Up Before Dawn

The neighbor's sprinkler,
the train echoing through downtown's canyon walls,
a soft persistent wind chime warning of whispers,
the ebb and flow of watery motor sounds
from the street below,
these pulsings of darkness are the
heartbeats of my early morning.

The chime, with fainter breaths,
tolls gently of insurgence,
the train, swallowed by the breadth of elsewhere,
is lost to a dream.
Softly the sounds of night recede
in the flooding light of consciousness.

Sharon Carter

GHAZAL FOR THE UNDERDOG

This one's a queer fish, they said, as it drowned
on the wharfside, gill slits gulping tangents of air.

Closet doors pivot on light's fulcrum—
inspection reveals nothing unspeakable inside.

True North deviates from magnetic North by several degrees.
Choose, and the journey becomes far simpler.

If we spoke in tongues, what message would we convey?
—it would be the patois of foreign spirits, an arpeggio of chants.

Foundation, mascara and blush, cannot conceal
violet hues—a cartouche where skin impacted skin.

Invisible dark matter holds the universe together, duping
white dwarves into believing they are the only show around.

A quarter dropped into a metal cup sings
more sweetly than a bottle top hitting the pavement.

We have forty-six chromosomes—the data bank of our differences.
When the sun sets, we are all scything the dark.

Andy Clausen

from THE OLD DAYS

I ain't saying I was brave but I stopped giving them the names
I hyped myself to know my body was not the end all
I prayed there were truths I would learn
that would be more important than my life my name
who I woke up to or with and who I saw
when I remembered my self fondly and temporary
and marveled perhaps
there would be no pomp and church feeling
when I comfortably ate and
loved and thought with the Noble Truths the blessed fruit of
knowledgeable womb the clear light of love as energetic as lust...
I worked in sawmills glass plants frozen fish packing hells and gandy
danced. I stacked hay, drove a cab and a limo, shoveled most of what
can be shoveled cement sand gravel clay loam sugar sawdust
manure snow & ice roofing shingles garbage concrete abstracts
frozen french fries pond scum dead critters coal I don't talk about
how I would shovel shit to keep my family while in my suit & tie
I sell Amway I really did shovel shit because someone had to do
it and I was good at it—was the manager
was the entertainment coordinator ran feature open readings in
Berk Ess Eff New Paltz San Jo Lower East Austin Jersey and
Boulder ran the readings at La Salamandra in 75-76
60 to a 100 every Monday Night feature—open and the old line
ups would have made you thought this was some pilgrim's site
some historical season, I did the Coffee Gallery and Minnie's Can
Do, Grace Cathedral and Folsom Prison's Greystone Chapel too,
How about St. John's the Divine & maybe 3000 or 30 years
before dodging rocks off the back of a pickup 1966
West Valley College? my first bar beer was in the Co-Existence
Bagel Shop North Beach when I was Catholic Hi-schooler and
and had not yet been introduced

to The Golden Eternity and I did a lot of foolish fucking and
worked at a plant extracting and smelting platinum from
automobile catalytic converter smog devices and got high lead
levels in Golden Colorado
and we pumped the sludge in a creek
goes down by the Arabian horse farm
but Rocky Flats was on the other side of the farm so what the hay
washed dishes at the Otsega where I got to behold Satchel
Paige's well chewed quid on a plate among thousands and I
picked frozen cow urine for a day and I grew a vegetable garden
that was acres and though the poetry promo police may have
little or bad to say about me one thing they can't say is I kissed
their ass, put it on my tombstone but I don't need no tombstone
on my grave all my life I've been a slave burn me turn me and
you know what I don't care but don't say I was a closet anything
not a bootlicker not some sex thing I'm out of the closet. I used
to be a very dynamic and intense face giver I would leave the
planet in couplings I never wore costumes though sometimes
tee-shirts and yes outdoors in magestical places, weird job sites of
quickies, & car seat nooners having sex happenings outside the
bedroom is not something I'll go in the closet about some of my
cruelties I'd rather forget and they were mostly mental and I
didn't tell myself they were cruelties but women were cruel to
me and sorry later on, I have the letters in my possession, when I
think of the immensity of the epical nature of my love I am
astounded how can a person like me actually be just some other
schmoe down the road some baggy pants over half century
hooligan scofflaw interview my lovers what smart and good
hearted, beautiful in everyway ask them for my weakness my
cowardly moments ask them if I have bad habits or leave the
toilet seat up, you want to know if I belong to secret
organizations? I don't like secret organizations, knowledge is to
be liberated I may have borrowed money and still not paid it
back but I never once felt I didn't owe it and I have been forgiven

and been ready to forgive and I hit 8 out of 9 one day 8 dollar
one dollar box and cleared 3100 out of 39 and lost 500 on large
bets and then walked out to blow the dough in other ways but
that was my biggest day and I hung out with & interviewed
Allen Freed's son Allen Freed a fellow cab driver in Austin and I
listened to John Steinbeck Jr. in the Trident Cafe "My dad said
learn the classics and the street so I'm a Greek scholar Buddhist
junky" our daughters were pals and he died and you may never've
heard of me you may mark my markings in the covert file of the
crazed if that's where you got to go that's where you got to go
find the old days

I was down to fragments shards slivers I was at the bottom of the
hole when the shovel would no longer reach was never blown off
a stage not even in Russia— my major organization takes place
in the wc and here's to all my friends give em a free pizza bill it
to the American Academy of Arts and Letters and I met Ralph
Ellison there Vonnegut Schlesinger and Christo and dined with
the widows of fleeting fame and on the other coast at the Great
University I sat with the Poet Laureate and the Nobel Prize and
the other literary teachers and lights and listened till we were late
for Me & Allen's reading (on & on about shop grants chairs
foundations: shop talk.)
and I want the secret joy I felt to go on forever
and I liked the beat when I had every reason to dance
I played ball with Rudy May Joe Morgan when I was 12 I saw
Sonny Barger on a bicycle I was there the day they made acid
illegal in California at the panhandle when we stopped traffic
with a dancing daisy chain and I sped with the speaker where
Janis was trying out with Big Brother and I was on a flatbed truck
screaming to sing it with a little more soul which is what the old
man told me after we returned from driving to the sun via the
Bay Bridge going straight in the air where I was eaten by the

parkling om and Solomon Burke was on the radio singing take
me take me and now I was preaching and the movie stunt
driving trips and crazed on the sidewalk and through park no
permission outlaw driving trip and my bodily functions could
barely maintain—I mean all of them—I thought I'd died
because what we were getting away with was impossible
and I've had good licks and lucks in Oklahoma I had no
advantages in my quest other than I was raised in Oakland
California and slaughtered in Chicago
and came from a very abusive and crazy make anything out of
Dostoevsky shoot it with crank it still can't encompass the totally
self absorbed & demented survivalist insanity of my
upbringing—I'm still in awe and denial and it's a story can't be
told I would explode
I'd go in the night like Tom Joad I'd be someone someone not
petty someone generous someone trustworthy someone heroic
someone else I had friends painters woodsmen hermits be-bop
drummers, writers hod carriers brick layers and actors and
sculptors and carpenters and priests and sikh do it wells, and
muralists and school teachers and ne'er do wells and fisher people
and travel writers and ecologists and lonely people and civil
servants and pseudo servants and suited servants and the chosen
necktied saints & barkeep bargain therapists, waitresses, don't
forget the dishwashers and the brooms, all those dead ones were
they editors did they run little magazines were they everywhere
you were last seen? I live inside cardboard I spring to life like a
spring and I helped rebuild the Parthenon in Garrison New York
and I could change the colors of Moran Wyoming sun leaving at
will green gold purple orange lavender silver all at once now yes
chanting Sa Ta Na Ma and more wonderful things happened as I
fulfilled 40th Century requests from an old (she's young) and
beautiful love and yes I slipped and skewed my back but that was
then and I'm back Jack & peyote & the lost highway no no

description of what a woman a stand up woman she'd become
just suffice to say it was good and go on
with the music don't say I overstayed
you just can't kick out the old days

And I saw them at the Cafe Babar where they had a poet's theater
for all a rough and tumble push it crew and told Bruce watch
give it less than 10 years, gone in all 4 directions, all 6, I've seen
this before you've got talent and I'll buy your book then I said
check out this cat QR Hand he's the greatest and I read at a
poetry and the people conference Rutgers and they knew I
wasn't a phony that did get me more than a bus ticket yeah I love
grueling bus rides after they're over, New York to Oakland in the
December and Kathmandu to Jiri, Chiang Rai to Chiang Mai,
Hanuman temple through coastal mountains to Goa, walked the
rope bridges of Solu Kumbu and as I was weaned I heard boish
delivered bombs explode up above where we lived
I drank the beautiful wine of the protector of the Corfu
Mentality rode on
every word bombed out of mind I had to do 500 lifetimes of
drinking in one but I slowed down after 50 or so and I ought to
donate my lungs to Hightimes, and all the outlaw standards pills
thrills chills caps bags balloons spoons bongs chews cookies
reapers cartwheels black widows
Hawaiian Baby Woodrose seeds Belladonna Buttons a bunch
ending in ol and al and ine and grimmies and vikes and perks and
brown and white and boy and girl and window pane and aspirins
and cartoon paper and calendars and black applesauce and
Oswalds and sunshine and haze all that just to get here and the
jobs fill in with 10,000 words just imagine and the good work.
And the macrobiotic diet and the total pig out and the hangovers
from this excursion I will surely pay but I just wanted to prove I
could live it again all at once that I could still handle the old
days

Clausen

And I counted beer and pop bottles and rolled my pennies well
after I'd seen a half century and sold an autographed to me book
by my dear friend and mentor for twenty bucks and lost it at
OTB and I sold my miniature carpet covered Fender Bass amp
for gas & groceries and I was a Rube early on and was burned by
an unjustly mythologized underworld and I got a buddy in
Hollywood in television who's bailed me out of jams and if I had
a few disciples and a pimp's heart I could be a spiritual teacher
and live off the labors of others and I'd have gifts instead of loans
and a job saving the ozone but instead hallelujah I'm a bum I'm a
bum who has to work to keep up with both his bad & good
habits, the good ones I suppose are the ones that keep me living
but the bad make a good case for that also, don't tell insanity is all
chemical, it was not chemicals that legitimized the insanity of the
Inquisition, The Holocaust, what was done in the so called
underdeveloped countries and given now forgotten names,
that insanity adds up to a lot, and don't ask me how I'm doing
unless you want an answer and I will no longer prepare a ready
answer why don't you ask me about the weather on that I am
much more glib and all you want to
do is be polite and I thought I needed more than that from you
but I was wrong cause I'm still here and on this won't allow
myself to feel bad, no harm no foul, no regrets no forgets even
what I've forgotten don't forget invade from my subconscious
torment me but don't let me forget and I can live on rice beans
oatmeal and potatoes for a long time and I broke a 20 day fast on
pizza and I've done the lemon juice olive oil Epsom Salts gall
bladder flush more than once and what were Big Z and I
thinking driving on into Salt Lake at dawn and just going on
Felton Calif to Boulder Colo in
23 hours and we had for real the best smoke in the world, I know
I know but people locked themselves in the bathroom & heaved
and it was only hash and kief from the mother plant that won the
all round prize at Amsterdam, Jerry smoked this bud man and

83

they tried to not like us in Boulder cause we hadn't learned our
chops the same way they did and also we were more than half
over as people and still not rich famous and that was embarrassing
to them but some liked us because we were the embodiment of
Pozor we were a reminder of what could have been we were
ready for a thousand thousand lays we were ready for a second
chance at the old days

And have I ever had visions of the women I've known in my day
being sexy and giving in to our love in the old days with the old
ways why yes I have had that type of vision always confess to
being blessed yes in these visions I never wondered if it was good
for her because that was the first given knowing by the motion
and sound in the garden of life our way which is the goal of my
practice to make God do our will and to always love who so ever
so loveth me for I represent danger the unknown the face you see
once in a crowd and turn away before I can and is that one look
the way you always say goodbye and I notice when the
gendarmes can't peg me for awhile I'm not defeated but I sure
ain't the regular style and I try and I try and pinch the inch that
will keep me blessed till they've had their fill of running around
the wall and invent the lie detector word processing program and
keep us going till the next paycheck didn't you realize you
signed off when you signed that list?
till my lips get numb and my eyes have black rose petals
and the litter ison the streets like a paste as an island way of life
without the bread and pretensions came out of the houses and
comedied the streets with remnants needed fruit trees is all and
I'd give a somebody else's million for a chance to be anonymous
again like a cosmic witness protection program where I'm the
only one knows my identity even God's census folk, lost track. It's
like a star trek episode where one finds out what would have
been if one hadn't been and it reduces the entire show to tears

and forgiveness—it is such a time of psychic healing that it's
immediately forgotten and danced and sung into the night with
Sergei Yessenin heckling into the night of The Persecutions of
Urizen. Allen Ginsberg & Bill Blake are chuckling. The white
electricity burns the midnight as the oil glistens on wing &
land—and I see the King Salmon fight up the falls by the library
on Ketchikan Creek I see the camel rocks of Seldovia and feel
the whiplash of the tiny prop plane over the inlet and Lucky
Hayden was the greatest dump man I've known and a very
Lucky pool player who once broke up a fight by demanding
silence "I have to shoot the 8 ball" shooting the 8 ball with a
starter's pistol he salvaged from the dump and I was one of the
organizers of a poetry reading that went 145 hrs. and 14 minutes
ended with Maya Angelou 263 poets yeah Bob Kaufman read
Second April in a dashiki as we followed with our texts and I
remember Paladin's wake and the last time I saw him and
Cynthia and Bob and Michael and that whole La Salamandra
season and I was there with E. Katz at the Roxie and The Shuttle
when I still thought we'd see the Big Change if we just worked a
little harder did it with a little more soul, and I was there with
Antler when they dedicated Naropa's Ginsberg library and again
four years later putting rocks on his grave, I hand dug a septic
system the fastest and delivered in the state that year and I took 7
Lorcets a day at 51 and drank a quart of T-Bird in 45 seconds on a
dare at 19 and my parachute was real and I hated the slithery
little machines that produced the cackling voices telling me
everything I thought was everything was a hoax with their
everything is a hoax mantra, the universe is a joke on you and
everything piece of Buddha matter is laughing at you at your
foolishness and weakness—
I took another toke yes a thousand thousand lays
back there in the old days

Linda Clifton

TIKKUN OLAM
The Repair of the World

Remember
inscribing
his
name
over
and over
in margins
and flyleaves?
Find them
so many years after
in Milton,
on school notes.
Remember
with your hand
tracing those lines
as if they were the planes
of his face, his smooth back.
That passion
to make him
be
in your world
with the press
of your pen
to smooth paper—
remember that.

Understand
this kind of faith.

Cathy Coan

MINNOWS

The soles of my feet love
the warm pine floor of your cabin
and you've left cold milk,
the syrupy smoke of dark—

roast beans, a window open
where the swelling sky, peaked
and hesitant with rain,
lights a glass bowl: minnows

who survived the bucket home,
darting, one night older. Miraculous,
alive, their delicate green lines
betray miniature fillets—too small

for pine nuts and wine, tougher
than tap water, this brilliant
captivity. Isn't it what
I've wanted, my whole life?

Sky Cosby

MY FATHER'S SOCKS

were woolen, warm
but under them
whole worlds of wisdoms.
that carved wood box
with a pen and a pipe,
I learned to scrawl my dreams with smoke.
tobacco tins with tiny candies,
batteries & radios,
ancient 1800s pornographic picture
yellowed curling edges turning
tricks towards my inquisitive
questing youth.
curiously thirsting for a signpost of some sort
I stumbled on the tumbled trinkets of papa's past,
wild years inciting child's tears
that stream and dream to dismal drawers.
baseball cards and bubble gum from 1972,
saint christopher choking beneath dusty wrist-watches
and moldy rubber bands.
cans of shoe polish, wallets musty,
silver dollars that lost their shine
so many socks ago…
when I was a dream in my father's pipe
and words were wishes in the smoky doom.

Cosby

When All Across My Skies

When all across my skies lie candied apples
surely comes the time when all we ask is what we need.
When kingdoms rain down on anthills
and abolish them to muddy ruins
cannot justice find some food at our so growing table?
The tides of violence have not risen so to block our sun of
common sense
for if the world changes to that degree
I don't want to be a part of her any more.

Sunrise—I watch my dreams turn dust
and vanish on the morning's breath
sending little shapes of what I used to be to sea and corners
of the earth I'll never see
and don't the good ones get remembered in decency and praise?
Never will I place my trust upon another
just to have it dashed away by seasonings
that I don't like to cook with
and someone told me once it isn't what we get from life
it's what we gift it back.

Noontime finds me seeking shelter from spring showers
sent to soak and soothe
in baths of booze some artists flounder
in my kingdom we have crowned her
muse of mishap, queen of questions, girl I mailed the box-tops of
my fantasies away to.
Youth, I sit and ponder the inconsistencies of dragon-flies
the randomness their logic weaves
on threads of air and strands of nothing.
Cleanliness is relative especially in bedrooms of the busily artistic

Cosby

who buzz and grind themselves to death
for men who never read their work
and women who pretend towards love while walking visions
of their own beside my bed frame.

Fade day's light my eyes peer endless
tasting of the fruit that was compassion yesterday
but now has rotted into indecision.
Twilight near-sighted and stumbling
raging our emotions on the stage of every day
but some don't realize our each action is our play.
Each whisper in the darkness an implicit notion held and
sometimes shared
with others so deserving of hot chocolate with their nightmares.
Some children wake up screaming
with the summer fear of life in them
as children they perceive this place as lacking sentiment,
too cruel and harsh a land to bide one's time in.

Fall of night brings long caresses
countless dreams of evening dresses
brushing back the night's long tresses
dreaming change and printing presses
a silver sky did greet me while I walked to work this morn
never did I think to ask it
          was it smooth or jagged torn?
          Considered it my heart forlorn?

Michael Daley

PLAYING CATCH IN HUNGARY

He wants grounders,
till one takes a wild hop
on ruts in well-trimmed grass,
an opening beneath the oaks.
"They're out of reach," he yells,
and fires above my glove.
I trot to yellow clusters
whose pungency lingers
on my throw, and brings me home
to graves and the rubble of jihad.

                       "Mit es?"
What's this? "Amerikaiak,"
say the strolling lovers
here in Szeged by the Tisza.
A little boy scurries and dives.
A white flicker in the grass,
a father in the field,
sunset tips the castles orange,
the rebuilt bridge a brassy wave.
Gold mine tailings
Australians paid Romanian
graft to overlook
brought cyanide to Tisza's beaches,
and to their famous bottom fish,
a hundred thousand mouths
of hairy spiky "oh's,"
as Szeged's anglers wept
about their poisoned catch.

He worries he'll be out of shape

Daley

next chance up at bat.
They know this, the lovers in the grass.
They see we keep our ways;
if we adopt Hungarian ease,
diamond and pennant will vanish.
They are very young.
It wasn't even their parents
who tried not to know
the millions in Nazi nets.
They're too young for so many zeros.
      An older sister,
Stalin's face a paint flake on a web
in her grandmother's story, gives me her hand,
eyes red, lashes glistening.
Vapor trails bloom and perish.
Twelve triggers armored
for an anthill in Jalalabad,
they streak the east and River Tisza.
A bloated sow belly up
is drifting down toward Belgrade.

He throws the ball perfectly,
but I'm already tired.
He knows I'll call it quits,
as my father knew,
relaxed in creased khakis
after thirty bombing missions,
when boys on bikes rode past
calling me to glass-strewn lots,
my scuffed ball exploding
in the dust beside his mitt.

Daley

THE PARIAH'S TALE

> *Flood tide below me! I see you face to face!*
> —Walt Whitman

When you ferry to a foreign country, when you walk aboard,
never carry anything. Your hands swing at your sides.
Let allusions to what you should have known hang in the air—
the fountain of antimatter, names of celebrities,
score of the game, life of a head-gasket,
source of pollution, flag of the state,
age of the Milky Way, size of a sturgeon,
invitations to sex.

The little island in the archipelago has a light for safety,
not enough there to build a tent
in the mouth of a strait to spare us.

The church and the schoolhouse are locked in the daytime.
On the big island the eagle circles the courthouse.
You could scavenge all your life the bones of our romance
with justice unfurled on a morning's swashbuckling breeze.

He dives into the wake of a gill-netter to steal from messy gulls.
One screams in beeline pursuit;
he strokes a mile or two over a sloop and pleasure boat,
over a meal of brine to perch, so picky,
on the far side of the southern island
long after the fisherman replaces his binoculars into the bucket,
and returns to his net.

If you were the unwelcome guest, harsh irritant below the skin
with that sour odor, if you, pariah,
spilled your bowl on the table

Daley

or dropped your pants to the neighbors,
if you never let go, dog on the cuff, if you chewed up,
and spat out the family peace,
you, an up and down bucket in a well—
to be useful shouldn't you,
ignorant of the ritual but mindful of what's expected —
spread your parts along the shore
and give your heart to the ants?
Over the rail the shadow of your head in the water fills with
white foam,
wake rides the rays of sun to your skull,
and joins your petty brain to vegetable flotsam.

Gone on a ride, you entered the alien zone,
innocently cruised the border of your own behaviors.
Who knows, for all the distance,
but I am as good as looking at you this minute?
Future generations, I spit here too.

To be helpful, should you plant a stake in the crevice of the tiny isle
and lash yourself to it?

                    Who will love me? Who will want me now?
Keeper of rock, oasis in space.
I have drifted so far from the map now everybody's angry.

Madeline DeFrees

THE PARADISE TREE

Framed in my window, this birch in winter drab—
long strands blown horizontal in the gale—
reminds me of a woman caught in dishabille,
weeping, of course, and clutching at her robe.
She owes her body to her sleeping husband's rib,
without him, would be incomplete, and still
her gaze strays outward past the farthest hill,
the stranger's word, she thinks, a shade too glib.

Knowing how soon the picture-perfect stales,
she's heard that virtue is its own reward,
a paltry one that turns the spirit slack.
Enclosure is the ambience of jails
and love's the angel with the flaming sword
who guards the gate, prevents her going back.

Jeni Nelson Delaney

A PRAYER FOR YOUR CAT SCAN

You would think one death's head
would meet our quota for this year—
a couple like us,
all coupling and joy.
Why should we have to shiver
and breathe the grave
twice within one year?
I would happily go back to when
you were the strong one
holding my hand.
This NOT KNOWING is hell.
We talk more and more as days go by
about time rushing,
white water rapids…
But in
NOT KNOWING HELL
time drags its tail—
dog days in death valley.
I bargained with God today—
impromptu bathroom prayer is the only kind I'm good at.
Last week you weren't worth a plug nickel
in your perfection.
This morning
I told God I'd take you in any form:
sick
blind
paralyzed down one side
unable to speak…

Delaney

I'd feed you
dress you
sit with you in every hospital room
in the western hemisphere
if He would just let you stay.

Rodolfo de León

THINGS THEY HAVE HERE
TO TAKE YOU AWAY FROM HERE

under the wan moon, no kindly smoke of incense
wreathes for you.
  —Nguyen Du

I.

With throat bared and clavicle broken
the evening star gleamed in the bayonet
on tender neckline,
a pulse exposed.
He begged for the corpse he was
to become,
begged not to be left
for the dogs.
Neither Red Cross nor Geneva will prepare his deathbed.
There is iron in his enemy's heart.
There is iron in his own throat.
Alone and unburied,
he will be forever wandering the sky,
tethered like a kite, subject to the winds
and fluttering between heaven and earth,
in the middle of nowhere,
while his family seeks his body
in the countryside.
Their empty house
will be burning for an eternity with incense.
The women will be heartsick.
The old men will name the fallen
one by one by
one.
And the night sky

will be their scattered abacus for the gathering.
The young men will smolder and taste ash in their
crooked mouths.
And the children will hide and jump out of the dense brush
with sticks in their hands, and scare each other
laughing
until sleep comes to end their play.

II.

Crossing from one side to another, now on his back,
he cursed the ground
cold and hard
as the pale, evening star flickered
above
like the lone traffic light in the middle of
his small town
a blinking yellow moon
with no business at all to exist over
a Main Street crossroads.
He thought of all he and his friend had done together, and all
they had gone through
on the battlefield
away from line company
on R&R.
Fire fights. Recon missions. Search and destroy.
Beer. Whores. Weed. White rice whiskey chasers.
USO shows, if they were lucky.
Movies in the club. High school memories. Waiting for
the news from home.
And church.
How long we gonna have this frog-stranglin' rain? his friend once
asked him about the monsoon season.
Another time, over beers, when he lied about not being a virgin,

his friend said: *You cain't piss on my boots and tell me it's rainin'*.
The last thing his slain friend told him
on the night of their last mission together:
Don't be scared. We all gotta die some time.
The tears were long gone.
Let the dead bury the dead.
At last, he rose,
breathed in the heavy, damp air that bogged him down
and waited for something, anything to happen.
With only numbness in his chest
and a piercing headache,
his head felt disconnected from the rest of himself.
He knew his heart had rusted because the
bitter, red phlegm
was trapped in his throat
like shrapnel.
Nothing remains
not even the remains.
It all goes.
They leave with the dust-filled air.
They leave in body bags.

III.

Rickshaws and mopeds
zip
as quickly as dollars are exchanged
by American tourists
in Hué.
The Forbidden Purple City
is gray as rubble
and there are no gates at
the seven gates into the garden.
The nine urns etched with

de León

sun, moon, meteors, clouds, mountains, rivers
that honor the power and stability of the throne
are bleak and bullet riddled
and the ashes
have gone the way of the grim dust.
The tourists take pictures
anyway.
A young man
an amputee
lies fast asleep on the sidewalk with
his unstrapped artificial leg
next to him.
People walk by, around, over him.
Cars honk bikes beep little boys holding postcards
catcall the foreigners
sizzle escapes from the street shops the police blow their whistles
as he snores
to the humdrum of
an everyday lullaby.

Alice Derry

WE WERE BOTH ABOUT TWENTY

I lay down in front of the draft office in D. C.,
didn't move from that acre of bodies
until they carried us away.
Paddy wagon. Fingerprints. Mug shot.
Disturbing the peace.

We were middle-class white college kids.
No one wanted to hurt us.
Released by 11 to take the bus home.

Not like the Black women in Montgomery,
boycotting the buses 15 years before—
meaning they walked miles to work, then walked home
to children and cooking.
I hadn't given up anything.

I pinned my arrest slip like a talisman
to my bedroom door and didn't do
civil disobedience again.

That's when you were in the war.
You never really told me,
but I've read enough: jungle's betrayal,
not sure if a five-year old you met
was the enemy.

You didn't die there.

When I was your teacher almost twenty years
later, I couldn't remember
the name of the man
whose candle I carried
that year in Washington,

Derry

50,000 of us,
each with a lighted candle for one of the fallen.

Even then I despised my lack of feeling for him—
that I would not properly carry
his torch through the years,
can't go now to the granite wall
with flowers.
Can't find you there, either, whose name
I could never forget,
your pages searing my stack of manuscripts,
the heat, the tall grass hiding
the years I had forgotten him.
I called you to the office—

Whatever you do, keep on writing.

It's so hard for me to come to class,
you said. *I get nervous in crowds.*
Three marriages and five children.
This last one, you said,
the only one when you were *straight*.
It broke up too: one small daughter
paddling her hands in April sunshine,
and then you were gone.

It's really best, your wife said without emotion,
come to tell me at the classroom door
half way through the quarter.
He needs more treatment.

We had those talks.
And you could write like crazy.

Nothing I could do
to hold you.

Derry

READING THE NAMES

And I'm thinking no one could read out
all the names of the Jews the Germans killed
or all the names of the Germans who died in Stalingrad's winter
or later—after the war—the names of all the East German women
who vanished in Siberia.

No one could read out all the names of the Vietnamese killed.

I'm standing at the podium
by the traveling Vietnam Memorial Wall,
helping to read the names of the dead
from the thick book of them,
each of us taking our fifteen-minute turn,
so by the time the wall
leaves our town,
we'll have read them all.

And because I wasn't taught phonics
in first grade—still trying
the whole chunk of the word—
I'm stumbling over my stint in the H's.
I start to use German—
where sound matches sight—
and then I realize
it's because these are all the German-Americans
falling one by one,

and a person wouldn't know
if they were the sons of Jews,
or of pacifist farmers
who witnessed the Revolution.

Derry

The breeze from the Strait begins to tear
at my pages, but the names rush on
whether I can pronounce them or no
my rolled *r* and throaty *ch* get thicker

and I'm thinking the names of the Jews *would* be German—
or Polish or French or Czech—
Germans against their own,

my hand moving the yellow card
down
to reveal the names
one by one,

and I'm thinking who here could
hold properly in their mouths—gently,
accurately—the names
of the Vietnamese?

I've been told to stop at *James Herbert*
because a woman wants to read out
by herself
the name of her loved one.

I'm over a page away from him
when I feel her coming across the lawn toward me.
I can't look up from the names.
I feel her standing there crowding me.

No it was *Hebert*, where I am right now.
She takes the card from me,
I feel my good shoes scrape on the cinder blocks
behind me.

Derry

I stumble out so she can read
her name,

but then I have to go on
reading.
Someone is holding her,
the names are coming,
why haven't I stopped to fold her
into my arms?

Why am I reading the German
names of the fallen?

They are waiting too.
They keep
forcing me forward,
to let these dead
be dead.

Brett Dillahunt

AMOXIUMPQUA

Abandoning Dave's red Chevy at the wash,
only the noise of thought and machine break the silence.

No one is here, and no one is coming.

Driving the bike up every hill and rise for 11 miles,
exhaustion, a broken wall.

We pass broken frames of cabins,
abandoned in the 20's when the timber wouldn't pay,
staring us down like gape-toothed old men,
folds of rotted bark and moss hanging from the doorway,
aged skin, fragile bones.

Amoxiumqua is up ahead,
seven hundred years old and waiting,
rising above the bend as we pedal the last few turns to the top.

I see Jemez Springs off the edge of the mesa.
Soda Dam.
La Cueva.
Tent Rocks.
Valle Grande.
Viewed from above for the first time.

My feet crunch sandstone,
no,

pottery.

Dillahunt, B

WASPS

Less adobe than plain mud,
the walls intersect at
crumbling corners
accented with rotting pine.

In the late morning (it is near noon),
you pawn the sleep from your eyes
for another sickened silence,
plant your ragged frame on the porch
and gaze jealously
at the houses built

of government meat and blankets.

Soon, you'll drink too much,
pile into the old Ford
and slam yourself through the village curves,
straightening the yellow lines
as much as possible,
pushing past your hunger,
until it's too late.

Spanish Crosses,
Descansos,
tell the story of your soul
leaving the body,
plowing and planting the petrified ground
of an old arroyo.

Dillahunt, B

The women have nailed them into the hard earth,
crying the rivers red,
filling your hair with sadness,
flowing through fingers like clotting blood.

And when the mourning is finished,
the Wasps pick your dried bones clean
of tooth and tongue,
flying blind on their way to heaven,
not unlike the tortured young
who sell your knuckles in the gift shop,
buy whiskey for the morning,

and gasoline for the old Ford.

Carolyn Calhoon-Dillahunt

To Bodeen, A Letter About Houses upon the Receipt of *This House,* With Thanks, as Always, from Carolyn

When I think of *This House,*
I envision vaulted ceilings, oak cabinets, a skylight,
built in bookshelves, a porch.
This is the house of my dreams,
the house I love at thirty.
This house will probably end up on a few acres in Zillah —
where we were supposed to have started,
between Franklin and Prosser High—
before grad school changed everything.

But what I am really seeking as I dream of This House
is Home.

For five years, I have been a nomad, a transient,
moving from work to school to work,
from house to house,
not moving far, but constantly changing –
before I can get comfortable?
Or abandoning it, still searching for home?

Of the five residences I've lived since being married,
none have been homes.
The closest to Home was 9th Avenue, where Brett lived while
student teaching and subbing—a dilapidated house,
too cold in winter, no air conditioning in summer, peeling
paint, a rotting roof—

but it was there we fell in love, so its appearance became
endearing and my memories of it always warm.
(I want more than I did at 23).

The series of addresses since,
mere storage units,
needing us no more than we needed them.
No lawn to care for. No fixing (the landlord's job).
No pets allowed.
We can leave for a weekend or for weeks; it doesn't matter.
Nothing will have changed.

We are ready to mow the lawn, plant flowers, get a cat.
To make This House into a place that's hard to leave.
A place, like a marriage, to work on together;
to clean, to fix, to paint, to furnish, to decorate;
to pull weeds, to plant trees, to water;
to love;
to look back on memories, good and bad, fondly.
Homes need maintenance, inside and out.

I envision This House, This Home,
full of light,
full circle (on a five year cycle),
where I sit on the porch, finally still,
on a summer evening,
watching my horses graze.

Pamela Moore Dionne

THE DEMOCRATIC WAY

In D.C., the House voted to impeach a president.
The official line was that he lied under oath.
This is not about sex, it's about law.
Censure was not punishment enough
for a Democratic leader whose Congress
had a slim Republican majority.

Meanwhile we dumped Newt
in favor of Livingston
who later declined speaker of the house
because his own sexcapade got leaked to the press.
He told us he would set himself as example for a president
whose indiscretions bore some similarity.
Representative Livingston, we presume
this means you lied under oath somewhere along the line,
since what you asked of Clinton could not possibly
have been *related to sex in any way.*

I got on every poll I could find. Joined anti-impeachment groups.
Phoned, emailed, wrote *Stop. Move On. Desist*…to no avail.
This Democracy grows less *we* than *them* and *us*.
Elected officials and the media think Americans
have sound bite powers of recollection.

That may be true for the collective *we*
but here is a promise you can stake your career on—
I will not forget.

duster coats. forgotten in
night in these words

← Back

~~Harison~~ Sheets

and present arms.
the caffine take
softly.
coffee.
to type things up.
wants a copy.
+ prose, built on cigarettes
coffee.
a kid asked me passing
hall.
soft a matter of

Jon Fischer

A CHAPEL UNDONE

Saw Michelangelo in a Tucson
alleyway, mountains curled around him—
lumpy old newsprint, discarded rubber,
articulate trails of his own
dampened chew. He got to town
on a too-late night, traded his Dodge truck for 50
bucks, cigarettes, and a bottle of Yukon Jack.
Same tee-shirt, same lavender
paisley flannel, crunchy with dirt, and a fetish
for sidewalk chalk. Scratching murals on a Zip's
burger-joint wall, joking with clerks
during smoke breaks, hash if they got it, or sips of whiskey
he drew angels in Levis, dazzled by atomic desert
mushrooms in a moldy pumpkin sky—psychedelic
if anything is. Maybe in heaven the cycle of angels spins
to the harp's peaceful ripples, but there is more
hell in Arizona, and the mix of car sounds, shoes slapping
hurriedly on the pavement, bitching doctors and grandmothers
is like a broken-reeded oboe on sunken breath. God stretched out
His left hand and seized him by the throat.

Joan Fiset

AMBUSH

Night.
Smoke rises.
He sets out.
Walks past the trees.
They are only trees as

he sits inside his house next
to the window, next to trees outside.
Inside his house he's grown watchful and uneasy.
This is called killing time because something out there
is moving through shadows no one else sees.

The chair is positioned for viewing the entire backyard,
every inch where darkness falls
threatens to keep a promise
whose sincerity he's never doubted
since the jungle taught him never trust
foliage, dusk, or the quiet hours where it looks as if
you're reading a book open on your lap
in your house at night with smoke on the rise
inside a house where no one else sees

how the sun no longer sets
as heat filters down
you smell the river.

He's in the river

Fiset

TAXI

Kneeling down to pet the dog
he said, I had two in Nam,
I was a scout, good dogs — one died,
couldn't bring the other one home.
He'd flick an ear: how many,
wag his tail: how far away.
Black shepherd, they couldn't see us.
I smoked a cigarette with a guy,
we put it out
then he was dead.
I've got to go now, but
up in the mountains
there's a place to fish.
It won't sound nice, but this is what you do.
Trap a small animal, knock it out,
slit the gut and hang it
close to the water.
Before you know it maggots
will be calling those trout to lunch.
Throw in the line then you're busy,
but don't take more than you can use.
I'm stronger than I look.
When they fit me for a flak jacket
ones my size were gone.
Mine was over three times too big
so I wrapped it twice around my chest,
when I got hit the bullets
left six bruises on my skin.
If I see you again I'll bring my dog,
Doberman and malamute mix.
Next door where I live they raise purebreds

Fiset

between a twelve-foot barbed wire fence.
When the Dobie jumped it
they wanted to kill the malamute's pups.
I said I'll find them homes and I did
but kept the one I wanted.
Got to go. Call if you need me—Car #3.
five a.m. to five's my shift.

Jonathan Fletcher

FAKE IT LIKE DEVOTION

Brass organ pipes every Sunday
and hymns burning up our throats.
Everything coming from deals—
with money—with
one last time.
Take everything from broken stained-glass
colors. Let your reasons thicken—
let them turn pink
and dull.

Shifting weight forward and walking.
Mistakes, stumbles,
forgotten mid-stride.
Foot down, and again.
Don't call it forgetting where we've been.
Call it remembering for yourself.
In gulps, drowning in heat—
dragging and pulling.
Giving in
like ignoring who we've been
and what it was we've said to them.

Shots of smoke and drags of honey.
Taking addresses like alcohol—
without history.
Chase it away
like summertime
like mosquitoes from smoke.

Carole Folsom-Hill

RULES!

Fuck the rules—I say
I say Fuck the rules!

This is crazy making.

Rules are not rules,
Rules are rules!

Crazy making hurts.
Crazy making kills.

Trapped, boxed in, blocked,
Breath is blocked.

Fuck the rules!
FUCK THE CRAZY MAKING RULES!

Breath is life.

Folsom-Hill

THIS PLACE

The core of me is this place,
the place where I am today.
It's the being of me, where it
all comes together.
It's the wholeness I yearn for.

Here in this place I am at once
hurry up, slow down.
Strong and soft,
impatient and patient,
loud and quiet,
aggressive and passive,
alone and together.

And there is more—
voice for those not yet ready.
Hear the voice of those who are.
Open the path for those in between.
See big and far.

Now in this place,
morning sunlight.
At the dining room table
silence holds the sound.
Hands moving on paper:
Enedina, Mireya, Magdalena,
Jim, Neli, Rosa, Luz and me.

The core of me is this place.
The place where I am today.
It's the being of me, where it
all comes together.
It's the wholeness I yearn for.

Greg Freed

HITLER'S CAR

I didn't know the word *genocide*.
I was only nine or ten.
I didn't know any Jews or homosexuals,
but my mom said our cleaning lady was a Gypsy.

I'd never seen a dead body
but I knew the difference between
a Panzer and a Sherman,
a Mustang and a Messerschmidt.

I recognized the uniforms
of the Luftwaffe and the S.S.,
the Iron Cross, the swastika,
and that mustache.

So it was with excitement
that I got into his car.

The glass was an inch thick.
I could barely open the doors.
They were armor plated.
I was told the thing weighed eight tons.

In the back, where he sat,
I sat
on the black leather seat.

It didn't smell like death...
It smelled like a museum.

Freed

The huge engine roared.
Then we circled the park.
I peered out of the unfamiliar limousine
into the familiar park,
perhaps as he had done
going through the Brandenburg Gate
to the Reichstag.

I don't know who his driver was.
Mine was my neighbor,
the millionaire who bought his car
twenty years after the Battle of the Bulge,
after the fall of Berlin,
after the Bunker.

I'd never heard the words
labor and *camp* used together before
but twenty years after the liberation of Mauthausen
I'm riding in his car past my home.

Fifty years after the liberation of Mauthausen
I'm standing within its stone walls
on a sunny day in the Danube Valley.

I'm squinting through the tears.
I'm gulping for air.
There's ghosts everywhere:
the quarry, the barracks, the ovens.

It doesn't smell like death…
It smells like a summer afternoon.

Freed

PESSIMIST

I have a nice house.
It is light and spacious,
welcoming and comfortable
durable and functional.
Except for one room
where it is dark and damp,
drafty and depressing.
A lone chair faces
a stained, blank wall.
The chair's seat is hard
and its legs creak.
For reasons that I cannot explain
I spend an inordinate
amount of time
in that room.

Freed

NIGHT SHIFT

As the final moments of my last night shift slide
from the future to the past
I want to assure the night that I bear no animosity towards it.
As this rosy dawn progresses I sense that I will not view dark air
with the same dread that has prejudiced me
this past twenty five years.
Perhaps I will view night as a home to secrets and romance
and not the broker of violence and fear that it has seemed to me.

When I commute on the silver train of night
it will be to go to the Museum of Dark Things
and not to labor in the mine
where dark deeds have deposited their ore.

And when I step onto the platform at Daybreak Station again
I will have my satchel full of dreams
and my hair at the angles at which my new night job has left it.
I hope that I will stop,
before hailing the bright yellow taxi of day,
and say a prayer
for the servants who empty the chamber pots of night.

Claire Freund

FEAR

The tiny little monster
he chokes your breath
quickens your pulse
creeping around
in the dark of night
hiding in the shadows.
Fear attacks you
in your most vulnerable
moment.
Watch out!
He's around the
corner.
Don't let him get to you,
or else he'll have you.

Hilary Freund

I SIGH

I sigh when I bake
a pie because it takes so
long so I sing a song.

Jeremy Gaulke

IN THE GARDEN
—*for Monica*

I pushed the rows apart
with my hands and two fingers
inch deep in the soil pulled
over the length of each mound
a place for the seeds I'd plant
too close together

I dragged you from the house
    before work
with mud on my clothes
and showed you how the corn grew
how the carrots grew
how the tomatoes
and the lettuce grew
I showed you in the garden
how the rosemary made my hands smell
  holding them up to your face
  and touching your lips
  with my thumb
I told you how the worms
got into the spinach
  leaving translucent carcasses
  trembling on the stem
how the fennel never had a chance
  how we should have started
  it inside
and how the pumpkins
were volunteering all over.

I went to the garden

Gaulke

like I wanted to go to you
my head in my hands
and my lips trembling
whispering to the basil
as I put my fists into the ground
how we always fought
and nothing was simple
how you never made love
to me anymore
       like you used to spontaneously
       in front of the bathroom mirror
       your panties around your ankles
       and half your make-up on
I told all of them there on my knees
in the dirt how much I missed the ways
we used to touch each other
       in the kitchen
       our friends in the other room
       laughing
       my hands around your waist
       while we made dinner
       for everyone

I saw you once, it was beautiful,
in the garden
stooping over the basil plant
your arms bare
in the warmth
of the last
of the sun
clipping herbs to give
to our neighbors.

Gaulke

I stood where you couldn't see me
watching your mouth hoping to see you whispering
like I did
everything you wanted
to tell me
in the garden.

I let the weeds later
spread over and choke
the corn full of earwigs and worms
the lettuce without shade
and not enough water went to shoot
the carrots clumped like mutant hordes
stunted and tangled with no room to reach
into the earth
I froze a bag of tomatoes before in a frenzy
I tore weed and vegetable indiscriminate
from the ground
letting only the herbs
remain to brave the autumn.
We stood where the pumpkins
used to be looking
over the nakedness together
I wanted to say to you in the silence
that this was your garden
that my hands moved the earth
for you
that everything here was for you
that I was sorry I let it die
that I had killed it
that every plant lay in ruin

Gaulke

I wanted to touch your lips
I wanted to make something
for you to taste
something to bring you back
to me.

but you spoke first and put
your arms around me in the twilight
"we'll do better next year"
pulling me back toward
the house away
from the wasted garden
and I went to you like I had
wanted to for weeks
and we let ourselves
fall back inside each other
the words hanging on our lips

we will do better next year
that now I know
for certain

Jack Gilbert

EVERYWHERE AND FOREVER

It pleases him that the villa is on a mountain
flayed bare by the great sun, and that all around
are a thousand stone walls in ruin (because
the farmers know as little of that old craft
as we do about love.) He likes knowing the house
was built by the king's telegrapher. *To Write
at a distance.* He keeps the gate closed
with a massive hasp and chain. The weeds inside
are breast-high around the overgrown rose bushes
and two plum trees. Beyond that, broad stairs
rise to a handsome terrace and the fine house
with its tall windows. He has excavated most
of the courtyard in back, and it's there they
spent their perfect days under a diseased
grape arbor and the flowering jasmine. There is
a faint sound of water from the pool over by
the pomegranate tree with its exaggerated fruit.
The basin is no longer choked by the leaves
accumulated in the twelve years of vacancy.
He has come to the right place and at the right time
to begin. But the silence still resists him.
The blue Aegean is far down, and the slow ships
are far out. Doves fly without meaning overhead.
But we are not part of them. Dogs and cats
know us innocently. There are meetings with a horse
we can misread into knowing. But we are singular.
If the universe perceives us at all, it's as objects.
Therefore are we so dear among the unconscious matter.
We alone grieve for our loss before it's gone.

He and the Japanese lady go out the back gate

Gilbert

and up the stream stone by stone, bushes on each side
heavy with moths. They come out under big sycamores.
There is a dirt path from there to a nunnery.
She says goodbye and he starts down to the village
at the bottom where he will get their food for a week.
The sky is vast overhead. Neither of them knows
she is dying. The last time he left before she
got back, she wrote, "Please don't wash your sheets."
Their bodies could hear each other beyond recognition.
On the return he thinks of their eleven years together.
Realizes they used up all that particular time
everywhere in the cosmos, and forever. He begins
to feel content with the separateness. To feel
triumphant, carrying the melon she wanted.

Gilbert

IS THE CLARITY, THE SIMPLICITY, AN ARRIVING
—for Judith Skillman

Is the clarity, the simplicity, an arriving
or an emptying out? If the heart persists
in waiting, does it begin to lessen?
If the man in the woods stands still
for an hour, will the bear forget him?
If we are always good does God lose track
of us? When I wake at night, there is
something important there. Like the hum
of giant turbines in the high-ceilinged stations
in the slums. There is a silence in me,
absolute and inconvenient. I am haunted
by the day I walked through the Greek village
where everyone was asleep and somebody began
playing Chopin, slowly, faintly inside
the upper floor of a plain white stone house.

Barbara Smith Gilbert

AN ON-GOING CONVERSATION ABOUT PLACE

Place does matter in that it can't matter
to platonic technocratic, technocentric
people
taught not to care
about place

because to care about place
would mean
to care about
HERE and NOW
disrupting systems determined
not to care.

From tribal meanderings and
sacred welcomings
to seasonal placed-ness
we are meant to wander while wondering
to wonder wandering
and WOOED into place.

Richard Gold

SAND

Fills the hollows of the zipper
      on your suitcase
Dusts a black sweater
Drifts at your door
Is buried in the towel
      you use to dry your hands

People who don't know they're
      unhappy together
People who have found one another
People who shield one another
      and themselves
People who love as friends

Mixes with the salt
      that clouds your window

The simplicity of love

Barry Grimes

AT THE HOUSE OF A FRIEND

The garden's snowbound.
Jasmine tea's served inside
in a flat metal pot.

Year's end approaches.
New Year's awaits, the same way
poets come to their faith.

30 December 2003

Two Chairs and a Table at Manzanita
—*for Tom Alkire*

Yesterday, the black fly's, there,
on the back of the pine chair
until the wind blows it along.

The beauty, the contrast,
the commonness, the uncertainty
of it all. Today, it rains all day.

Basho says, The skylark sings
all day, and the day is too short
to chop vegetables by mealtime

if the morning walk is taken,
past where the blackberries are picked
back from the road that ends there.

There are lines that don't work off each other.

Clouds roll around Neahkanie
past Manzanita and the mouth of the Nehalem
to Rockaway and the rest of Oregon.

Two women talk on the radio.
As they do, clouds show the trail
that cuts a line across Neahkanie.

People walk coffees and pastry to the beach.
The ocean air even softens the crackers
in the cupboard. The women finally play a song.

Grimes

David Smith, the metal sculptor, traveled to Italy
to work in a foundry. With his steel-tip boots,
he toed chunks of iron and steel into place

on the floor of the shop to get his lines right.
The foundrymen watched him and made him
one of their own at the shop and in their houses.

There is no skipping the playing around
with lines that won't work off each other.

The women on the radio get from Janis
to Ray to Bob Seeger's *By The River* line.
Seeger sings, I took my young son to the river.

I held out his young hands to feel the rain.
Seeger stops and guitars take it to the end.
One of Leonard Cohen's women, albums ago,

sat wrapped in a white towel at a table
by an open window with wood shutters.
She was turned from the table and typewriter

to us. The table, here, is pine, bare pine.
Cohen's table seemed made of planks
from an old Greek dock, as remembered.

The floor, here, is the color of the ocean.
These hands and fingers are soft and tan.
Neahkanie's buried in clouds, again.

Grimes

A bungalow sits back in the pines
behind a front yard of loose sand.
There's no sidewalk to the front door.

No matter how much the thumb of the same hand
plays with the three silver bands on the ring finger,
family, work, and poetry, they do not slip into place.

With the urging of that thumb the pen
also rests upon, the bands revolve,
three separate, silver rings

working off each other. Trinity.
Neahkanie means place of the gods,
highest coastal point between Tamalpais

and the Columbia. Two mountains and a river.
Hakuin says, Make the mountains, rivers,
and great earth the sitting platform.

Flat as a table, perhaps. A man who lived alone
on many rivers, and finally in a cottage gifted
by a shipyard and located on its ground,

wrote, I wish a cricket would sing.
And sing & sing, and know why
men go to live on cold mountains.

A man, who years ago caved in
to young poets who did not want to study
form, content to consider their own thoughts,

Grimes

says in a recent poem, among other things,
The way to whatever matters begins/
where you forget words and put down your pen./

He ends his book in praise of Cold Mountain,
Chinese hermit poet. Only the poems remained/
scrawled on the rocks and trees./

Nothing's undoing among/
the self-stung unfolding of things./

Two chairs, one taken, one empty,
and a table. Hands on the table.
One, three silver rings; one ringless.

Grimes

AFTER THE FLOOD

A long-legged teenage
blond farm kid
in old Levis and T shirt
yellow and white
feed company ballcap
squats on his heels
at the edge of the river
forearms resting
on his knees
his big hands and long fingers
hanging from his wrists
like blades on a tiller
says to no one in particular,
I saw it all last night.
Man said more than once,
Aint no body lost.

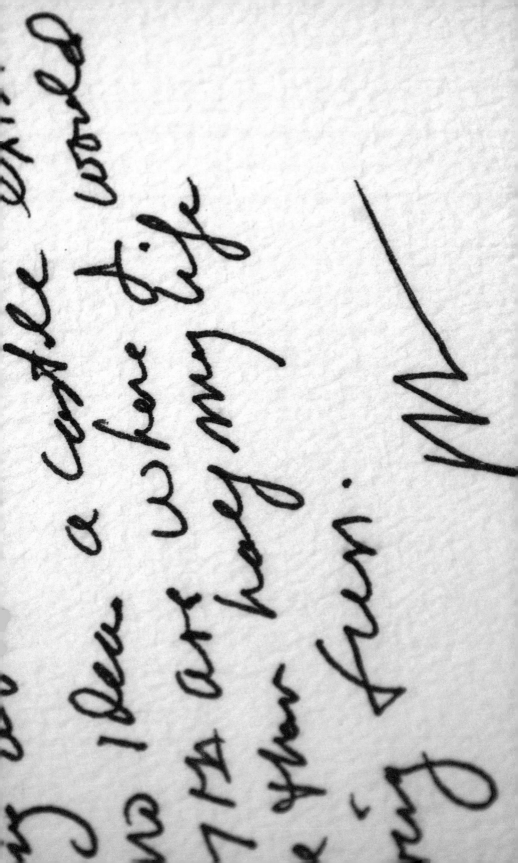

Sam Hamill

THE NETS

Somewhere someone is untangling
the heavy nets of desire
beside a small fire at the edge of the sea.

He works slowly, fingers bleeding,
half thinking, half listening, knowing
only that the sea makes him thirsty.

Jim Hanlen

HEALTHY STONES

Stone is just skin; all the pebbles, toes.
Sometimes you can hear the mountains
dance. In spring they seem to move
closer to town. Check their shadows.
In the place where mountains meet
other mountains, creeks carry
noisy messages.

STONE LANGUAGE

is the oldest. wind, forest and stone
were told to speak their language
to others.
            fire's language came later.
it had to be translated by forest.

stone would leave tracks. if you pick them
up, you can read the impressions.

wind leaves its tracks in the sky.

Hanlen

Kinds of Unwanted Stones

Pasture stones,
ugly stones,
witness stones,
some orphan stones,
stones without center,
stones that crush easily,
stones that won't crush,
the coffee brown stone
    if it's missing the gold flecks,
stones that don't make flowers look good,
stones that make creeks sore,
stones that have their nose in the wind—
    they seem inaccessible to climbers,
skin your knees stones,
and the ones Olga wouldn't put
      in her mouth when she was little
      or in her pocket now she's older

Stone Wisdom

Bees don't bother me, poisons—
no effect. Thirst, I've given up
and now there's no need. Standing,
sitting or lingering, I can give you
the low down. A blink or wave
that's another matter and never mastered.
Slugs, spiders and snakes are
no problem. My dry throat does make
it difficult. Now the guy who comes by
to set near here might have something
to say.

Hanlen

REPORT ON STONE

Your mother said you'd
never amount to anything.

Creek passed you by years ago
and it seemed like today.

Clouds seem to pass
without noticing you.

Mothers can be like that—
mountains with long shadows.

WHY STONE TELLS THE TRUTH WITH FACILE DETACHMENT DESPITE THREATS OF TORTURE

No fingers to pinch in a vise.
No penis to attach electrodes to.

Hanlen

STONE'S WRITING

A scrap,
a piece of life broken off,
bruised escarpment,
a cascade,
forgotten,
a misery of stone.

THIRD EYE OF STONE

After the other eyes failed,
all attention turned to the third eye.

Hanlen

ALL MY CREEKS

The creek that once was on my roof.
The creek that comes out from under rocks.
The creek that is mother and mouth.
The creek that is child and breast.
The creek that moves in my heart.
The creek haunted by cold and shadows.
The creek that moves in four directions.
The creek that can say here and there.
The creek that moon rubs its skin against.
The creek we can all enter.
The creek young men cross over and return old.
The creek guilty in spring, lazy in summer.
The creek that makes its own weather.
The creek of perfect pitch.
The creek that belongs here and now.
The creek heard in the sleep.
The creek that carries the universe.
The creek remembering itself over and over.
The creek willing to fill my bowl if I accept.

Sharon Hashimoto

Interned in the Heart of the Country, My Grandfather Searches for Fossils

Watching the dust scurry away
from his feet, he must have thought
of the weight of waves
as they curled, then flattened
into a ripple and how the sun always floated
to the surface in pieces. There, in Wyoming,
pale sand could have slipped
like silk through his fingers, leaving
the fossil in the palm of his hand,
the empty print of a conch
still hard and precise
where the long grooves once fluted
the water. Turning from the mountain
to the flat yellow land, did he feel
the slow drift of tides
surround him, the horizon pressing
miles on his eyes? Perhaps
loose grains of stone crumbled at his touch
when he glimpsed the thin pole of his shadow
pointing east. What did he look for
on the long journey back
as one step followed the other?
Years later, my mother would tell me
how she'd lie awake in her narrow cot
and wait
for the small sounds of her father's return.

Josh Henretig

HAIKU IV

Oh, turtle-shaped soap,
How you wash me with such ease—
You were a bargain.

Kristin Henshaw

In Late Winter

When you are dead
I will still search the gardens
for snow drops and crocus,
pull aside strands of grass, rediscover
fat heads of hyacinths, flat fingers

of daffodils inching out of winter,
buds still underground.
Gray whorls of columbine
will surprise me once again
when I think *winter*

in wet morning snows.
On your birthday in February
I'll find tight bouquets of primrose waiting
to unfurl their crinkled leaves
held close against the earth.

Not until March will I find
thin curling pencils
of poet's narcissus
multiplying on this coast
far from your Pennsylvania garden.

I will stand beside them
in spring sunshine
and wonder if I have stored you
in bulbs and tap roots.

Kitty Higgins

SEEING YOU TODAY
—to Bill

He was dying, I knew that.
Pale eyes, yellowed and drowning,
His face had a thin layer of life
Over the framework that would remain.
They said he should be gone by now,
I willed him to go when he was damn well ready!
What was he thinking?
Why wasn't he fighting?
"Take me out with my boots on!"
Where did the cowboys go?
Get the fuck out of bed.
Make me feel safe.
This is about me seeing you.

Abbey Howell

FRIENDS

—*9 ¾-years old*

Friends are nice, friends
are someone that will stick up
for you, even when they're small.
They can still stick up
for you, even if you're a big
kid, go ahead step right in. A
friend is someone that will not
hurt your feelings. If they do
they need to say sorry.
But....try to be a friend
no matter what, ya!

Janelle J. Howell

MOMENTS

I am twenty-three,
walking your lab
under pipe suspended
from the Shell Oil refinery
in Anacortes.
My 9-passenger station wagon,
safe enough for any daughter,
docked where pavement
meets bay.
I am searching
for a skipping stone,
clams for the grill.

Holes crumble and cave
with each scoop, lift, and turn.
Bo keeps people
cautious,
chases sticks, gulls,
beyond a shout.

In those moments
where tide is neither
here nor gone,
thoughts pull hand over hand
like words of a song
familiar, yet forgotten.

What I remember is this:
Your thick fingers folding
over my 5 year-old hand knuckled
like a butterclam

Howell, J

deep in your palm.
The sun rising over Diamondhead
through the hair
on your right arm.
Bouncing on your knee
to the chug of the tractor,
mud chips chopping air,
the steering wheel
too big to turn.

Standing in your boots
a size too large,
I want to know
your story, Dad.

Searching bubbles
in the slip
is a telling of truths
beyond what I can see.

The tide circles
my surprise,
taking your boots
beneath the surface.
On hands and knees
I reach in
beyond elbow,
grasping one boot,
then another,
pulling them free.

Howell, J

Bo meets me
at rippled edge.
We turn and watch
tracks disappear.
A passing boat breaks bow
against wave,
moving along the grain
of pain and regret.
Water bends light
to sky spilling
over my face, arms
open to wind
breathing me home.

Tony Hunt

LETTER TO BARRY GRIMES AFTER READING HIS LETTER TO ME ABOUT READING GARY SNYDER'S FORTY-YEAR POEM... *MOUNTAINS AND RIVERS*

Remember, Barry, I'm a hell of a lot older
than you are. I'll be fifty-seven in December.
Life in the slowing-down zone.
You're only fifty.
Snyder's sixty-six, forty
spent drawing the talkative peaks,
            the articulate valleys,
                        the mellow flow
                                    of the desert,
the emptiness invested in all.
I've spent twenty walking his trails
            barely any on mine
nothing to show except time.
How we go on. Kissing the mind
in the net that we share.
Ah…what's in this pack that we carry?
What's that flute player playing?
The love for an utterant airing of
language, for any one's perfectly
felt sounds given in shapes of delight.
Your letter delightful.
Snyder's poem a gift, graceful,
ideas shaped by the tones that we hear:
that he hears, that I hear again
and again as I read as you do…
We share.

Paul Hunter

WASH TUB SATURDAY NIGHT

Not always Saturday but mostly
when the tub clanks in from the shed
where from one week to the next
it hangs up out of the way

till the curtain gets pulled in the pantry
as the stovetop kettles and pots
steam up the windows
so little need now for drapes

the air gets sultry and hot
as we dig out our clean clothes
study our blisters and bruises
get ourselves ready to wash

with the kitchen lamps all ablaze
the hand mirror passing around
a little snipping and scraping
away the worst before and after

as in no particular order
depending mainly on need
one at a time we slip in
past the curtain strip and shiver

crouch naked in the tub
lather ourselves in all the hairy parts
then at last call out to another
to splash warm water down over us

Hunter

as we lean back eyes closed
cleansed head to toe
as if in a modest baptism
rinse off the last of what ails us

and when all have had their turn
shared that feeling pounds lighter
hair and fragrant blossom of the head
drag the full tub sloshing to the door

heave out into the night
the week's dirt and exhaustion
where for a while in the yard
it steams and shines

Connie Hutchison

AFTER STAFFORD: MY ASSUMPTIONS

1.

Every poem is a weather report:
how the soul is doing,
what milepost, what features of sky,
what marker was left yesterday
for travelers coming after,
for today's necessities.
A poem is one part of the self
speaking to another; writing a poem
is every day's *axis mundi*.

2.

Everyone feels, but we're covered
in layers; everyone excavates.

Children are most like kites.
The word is *permission*.

The Word is permission to love;
the body a cabin on the road to home.

Open all the doors and windows!
That unidentified bird on the roof,

the one you can only hear,
may be a rare owl.

Cherryl Jensen

BROTHER

The skin is stretched tight
over his swollen feet.
Black scabs, where the skin is dead,
mar some toes.
On others, open sores
ooze watery red liquid.

He lifts his left foot slightly
from the black metal footrest
of his wheelchair.
I gather the white cotton sock
and slip it over his toes,
push it back and up on his heel.
He puts his foot down.
We repeat the process with his right foot.

I circle each leg with the smooth black leg covers,
making sure the dip fits under the back of each knee,
then stick together the Velcro closures.

He struggles into his fleece jacket,
one arm at a time.
I stuff it down in the back,
where he can't reach.

He smiles at me
as he fumbles with the zipper,
his giant hands clumsy from the neuropathy.
He pulls on his soft leather gloves.

Jensen

I lay the green wool blanket
across his lap,
tuck it in at the sides,
around the edges of his legs,
under his feet.

We are ready to face the day.

YOU, ME, HER, AND US

The fat bitch
has a protruding stomach,
cottage cheese thighs
lined with spidery veins,
ponderous, floppy breasts.

The saint
has skinny bird legs,
flat stomach,
bony butt,
breasts too small
to fill a bra.

The fat bitch
talks with her mouth full,
beef and mashed potatoes
with gravy and carrots
mashed together
in a gray slop in her mouth.

The saint picks at her food,
one bird bite after the other.
A bit of potatoes, a slice of carrot.
Closes her mouth and chews
completely before she speaks
softly.

The bitch cleans her plate, mops
it with a piece of white bread,
getting every last lump of potatoes,
every swirl of gravy.

Jensen

The bitch
drinks beer out of a can, gulps
it down, wipes
her mouth with her sleeve,
belches.

The saint
drinks white wine
from a thinly-etched crystal glass.
Small sips,
making one glass last all night.

The fat bitch
runs through the house,
laughing, screaming.

The saint,
using sharp, stainless steel knives,
cuts that belly,
whittles those thighs,
chisels that face into angles and hollows.

She molds
the body toward
gaunt, perfect paralysis

while the wild, fat lady
smirks from her perch
on the swing—
smoking a cigar and
guzzling a beer.

Chelsea Johnson

THE PERSON I AM

The person I am
is someone I don't know,
someone I want to get to know.

Every day a little bit of that person comes out to
speak what she has experienced.

All the advice she has received has been recycled
for more than it's worth.
I've thrown away the ugly parts but yet I still kept
the experience.

It hurts and my body can
barely face its spirit.
My body cannot handle
my spirit's emotions
so it cries for help.

There's something my spirit wants.
It had that something
at one time but then it left.
So my spirit waits and waits for that someday
when that something returns.
Until then my spirit panics,
it flies wildly all night and all day.
Waiting, searching while its body cries.

My spirit has experienced
many things and the only thing
that can scare it is being alone.
Being alone all day and all night.
And knowing that
it could be worse.

Doug Johnson

WHALE SKIN

*It was my allowance - for ifI lived I would be one of the holy –
Holy Holy Holy Lord God Almighty - I would be pure/chaste/worthy—of
the terror—the heart/the hands across my skin/peaceful madness—of the
sleepless nights—of the sights—UNSEEN of the ever present spook
haunting my dark nights—deep. —Krystal Johnson*

Hospitals will forever be places of horror for me, little sister.
When you went in for a biopsy, we were entering a dark forest of
beeping tubes and white hollow trees called nurses and doctors.
The lady taking your blood couldn't find the vein and I wanted
to punch her. She poked your arm 3 or 4 times and you just
smiled quietly and said it was o.k. I knew then that no one was
braver. I was about 14 or 15. You had dealt with all of these
hollow trees longer than I had. You knew that the woman would
get it eventually.

There was a girl in the bed next to you, and your spirit forced you
to be more interested in her than in your own condition. I
wonder if she is still alive. I saw a documentary on a whale that
was beached and how some scientists were cutting into the blubber
and making sure to show the cameras the depth of the fat and all
of its reasons for being and hoping that the camera man was
getting their good side so that the world would know that they
were the smartest people with glasses and grey beards in all the land.

That girl was such a whale, though not quite dead when we saw
her. All five of us shuddered inside for the fear that you would
become that. She was 13 and you were 9. She was hooked up to
I.V.s and whatnots and smiled weakly as you spoke. I only saw
her in the shadows because I was not allowed in your room.
Dad bought you this big Teddy Bear because you were so brave.
We hoped your kidneys were o.k. from the prednisone. That's
why you were there.

Johnson, D

LOOPIE'S HIDE

I spoke with a man about my lupus and he was surprised and said, "You hide it well." And now I sing in my mind "you hide it well, you hide it well." A chant.—Krystal Johnson

Swing low, sweet chariot, comin' forth to carry me home.

Used to sing that together at the piano the days after Thanksgiving. Thanksgiving night they would all gather at the piano and sing. Harmonies blended that others couldn't hear. We would all hear them every Sunday morning in the first service. Remember the first service where there were no instruments allowed, but the only person there that could start the song was Dad?

Swing low, sweet chariot, comin' forth to carry me home.

There was not much to hide in the little church. There was you, and Susie and Sansie, but I can't spell her name right. Susie was blind and slow. Sansie had a stomach disorder that made them give her special foods. She was slow, too, and her parents still take care of her. When we were kids the little church couldn't start the song without Dad, and every single Sunday that Earl James was alive he would request "Immanuel's Land." I think it was number 101 in the little black hymnal. People ask why I can hear harmonies now, and I tell them instruments weren't allowed in the first service so we would all find our parts off of Dad. Sometimes he would sing tenor and we would find them there.

If you get there, before I do, comin' forth to carry me home.

But there was nowhere to hide without the instruments. Everybody sounded awful except Dad because they couldn't find the note. They always said your voice quality was like Grandma Johnson's, but even with most of them knowing you had lupus, they still looked at you like you were Susie. Susie had perfect pitch and would yell, "That's wrong! They're off!" at the soloists during special music. We used to sit in the back and giggle. She would listen for a person's voice before she would talk to you. You only had lupus, but they still looked at you like Susie. Susie had perfect pitch and yelled at the soloist.

Just tell my brothers that I'm comin' too, comin' forth to carry me home.

Johnson, D

HEALED

This is what I am getting my training in, not business, not psychology, but my health. I talk about going back to school and getting a profession, but I wonder if I will be able to actually do this. I am taking a class right now that requires no homework and isonly three hours a week and that is too much. I am exhausted for days afterward and must rest on the day I go or I will be wiped out. This is my life this is my bag—Krystal Johnson

Today I am healed as I tear shingles from a roof. It is 100 degrees and this is the last of the old shingles made of tar and modern invention. Epithets are spoken too loudly. We want the wind to agree that our words are equal to their rage, but they fall on dead echoes. They absorb into to the plywood sheeting that will hold the new roof. The knife I use to trim tar paper and new shingles in delicate new patterns was first held when Thomas was building a 12 year old's hunting crossbow that he found designed in a book from his first junior high in America. He gave me the knife to help me feel important in the craft, and get me out from under the makings of the bow. I whittled with the blade toward my hand and gouged my 9 year old thumb right. He tried to tend the wound, but spent most of the time trying to convince me to tell Mom. There was company that I never saw after that day—I was terrified they would all call me stupid for cutting my hand. I snuck up behind Mom's chair and tried to whisper what had happened, and she bolted out of the chair so that the entire room asked and had to look at the cut. Mothers are good about doing that. Everyone gave hometown wisdom as to whether or not I needed stitches, but when I dug my heels in and cried tears in the bathroom. She compromised and put on butterflies. Some old woman spent the rest of the afternoon chiding her to get stitches but she let me play, and I was relieved. Not letting the butterflies do their job, I pulled them off too soon expanding the scar. Today I'm healed and drink ice water after I'm done with my epitaph on the roof of 100 degrees.   It cares not for my words, absorbs my strength and I pound the last staple in to have the last laugh. It will hold a new roof. Today I'm healed, and roll the scar between the tendons on my thumb when I'm bored with the conversation.

John Johnson

THIRTEEN

3 Presidents
2 Principals
5 Football coaches
2 Fleetwood Mac Reunions
and 13 Poetry Nights in 13 years

It sprang from *Spoon River*
Bodeen had a poem about his father
Prout and his photos were pioneers too
Sometimes we had two a year
Sometimes it's hard to do even one

The only constant has been the voices
The fifteen-year-old boy new to the night, new to the country
The seventeen-year-old girl who held us all hostage
The fifty-year-old man who showed us poetry in the hallways
The Davis readers, one and all

Next week the Davis students take the state mandated tests
We should mandate our politicians to write a poem
Bring it here, show us who they really are
Mandate this you hypocritical dealmakers!
This is poetry night at Davis High School
It's about real kids, it's the real test

Lightfoot says we're all poets passing through
Grimes says it's about the kids, it's their night
The Davis readers say it's about time
Now the words will fly through the air like chain lightning
Now the ears will prick to hear a single voice
Mine, yours

Johnson, J

It's the thirteenth annual gathering
It's time for explosions in the head and heart
It's time to release the poems and let them run free
Long may they run

Laurie A. Kanyer

JARS OF TEARS

Fiction becomes our reality;
we are unified in our fear.
We are unblessed by microscopic fragments
and remains.
No plot is as unfamiliar as this place of grief.

Answer the call of the Eternal.
Can you hear His thoughts?
He seems to be silently shouting.

Lean into relationships
for a chance at reckoning our souls,
for what we can contain.

Grieve forming cerebral pictures,
or wailing lamentations.
Carry cemented jars of tears, striking
memorials like mountains and lakes.
Stack rocks in cairns to reach the heavens.

Shape promises, no matter how wide a swath
suspicion might plow.
Evil will not furrow over our thresholds.
Remember, you know who lives there.

While the earth may shudder, choose to plant
seeds of expectancy.
Invite the hills to sit as judge
and be rooted as memorials.
Disaster cannot level terrain
without permission!

Kanyer

You might strike cryptic symbols
as your testimony.
I'll make chalk marks on black parchment,
for we are not called to
silence in an unjust world.

Be one with the Holy, no other action could
express such pure intent.
For when you leave, evil shall not know
you've walked away.
Now count on art to illuminate
what we do not know.

For what we do not know, we do not know.

September 2001

Gayle Kaune

CLUSTERS OF STARRY WHITE FLOWERS

Cinderella must have had muscles
otherwise how could she shovel the stones,
bleach the hearth, use an anvil for a chisel?
And when she snapped the stems of vines,
clipped the climbing peas, chopped
onions for soup, did she bury her rage
like women of the kitchen,
her words clotted
by the thimble of her sex?

A prince will always be a nemesis,
taking courage away in a pumpkin coach,
placing his hands on the white pedestal
of her breasts when no one is looking.
And she, so charmed
by this fiery bowl, bracelets her escape
by this touch, elbows her way into the heart
of old godmothers who forget, who want to forget,
what while young women dream of escape,
they're trampled by rising hooves.

Tina Kelley

HAVING EVOLVED FROM TREES

We are hazel-eyed.
Some things we are certain of:
sun in the forest adds extra rooms.

We hide inner twisting under our skin.
A beehive within is a blessing.
Never play with matches. Ever.

We teach: to bloom, to fruit, to peel,
to heal in a swirling burl,
to suffer pruning silently.

We remember the itch of chickadees,
blue air of twilight like a shawl,
the liquor it resembles. We taste with whole selves.

Our women are never too stocky, don't diet.
Our day — dressing, bedding down — is a year.
At weddings we wear wrensong tatting in our hair.

We converse in the pulses of rained-on leaves.
Our god is wind. We need no heartbeat.
We worship by swaying, masts in a marina.

Our low song, too low, withers and flaps.
We sanctify the privilege of embrace,
of running, the afterlife of dance.

The sun pulls life through us,
up and flaring, a yellow scarf
from a magic tube, higher, wider.

We die with loved ones, rot in their presence,
nourish their offspring and watch
the continuance, ever, exulting.

Cal Kinnear

UNDERGONE

Winter sun under-
gone—
spent stain
left.

Unspeak-
able dye of
last light.

By inklight
at the touch-
hole,
night kindles.

Kinnear

PSALM

Psalm, *o*
gloria, o gaudeamus.
Sing, sang, sung.

Salmon, up–
current homing from no–
wherever.

Psalmon, un–
sayable word,
giddy
with collision.

Kinnear

Post

Weather-patched paint, brown,
dirt-brown, weather-, wind-
flaked, grainworn,
old wood, rain-stained, green
moss-stained, ocher rust-spotted, old
same wind buff and saw, gale
skyvast, skin-near, sea
weather-patched, flung,
gray wind-flaked old
sea, old cold sea.

SHIP OF (NO) STATE

A cantor intones Yizkor over the midnight water.

Hull down, running without lights,
a cargo ship passes,
the ship of oblivion, loaded

to the deck with semi-automatic weapons
packed in wood shavings and grease

for whatever new war wants them.
It plows a long, straight furrow. Racked on deck
are all the disinterred dead,

their good skins
tanned and cobbled
and boxed

one size
fits all.

She is
a ship under
no flag.

Where has the grief gone, carried off
on the wind?

Grief under no flag.

Klipschutz

THE EARLY BIRD CATCHES THE WORLD
—*Dateline Walla Walla, WA*

The philosophy chair from Whitman
roller blades circles around us
in a black beekeeper's mask.
We're here to greet the dawn with Charles Potts,
on his weekly constitutional up Mill Creek
to the Army Corps of Engineers Dam and back.
Elderberry trees along the asphalt path bear fruit.
Herons, mallards, cranes, Sunday solemn,
Sunday silent. It's we who can't shut up.

Bukowski is a tough sell with Jensen.
Potts piles on, aslant. He wins. He gloats.
Roethke may be royalty up here,
but Charles leaves him stranded
up a hundred year old beech tree,
crooning *Look at me* to birds of prey
in Nelson Riddle time. And then there's Larkin—
off the grid, a blighted branch, a windless bag!
Potts dismisses Ionesco, tosses Corso in the creek.
His lawyer cycles by, that lazy sonofabitch,
a September streak chasing October.

We departed in full dark, the risen sun
sheds reams of light. Charles unspools a yarn,
about a prison guard, his guilt, his suicide.
Clueless, back from two years in Japan,
Charles sees the widow and says, *Say hello to Monty.*
"Her face looked like I'd slapped her."

Now the day.

Zack Krieger

WE ARE TORTURING

We are torturing.
We are what we do.
Write a letter to a senator.
Not enough.
Think clearly.
Answer the question.

Dan Lamberton

ALL WINTER

All winter you studied for this
spring's seasonal flowers,
for perennial colors and you rejoiced
over the catalogue that named,
completely, the genus and species,
and you said to yourself, "oh"
and "just wonderful" and felt each
warm day was a certainty
that nothing would freeze out there
again, and, in your dust covered, mustard
colored jeans, you'd get down on your
knees and promise the ground
your fidelity too, and you were
shining. I thrilled to you. I will spend
all this spring planting, all
summer watering, all
fall covering, encouraging,
protecting, all winter learning
the next garden's words, dreaming
of you, out there on the ground
kneeling and saying "wonderful."

Joy E. Langley

A STATE

Johnny Jump-ups
create a purple haze over fledgling grass.
Yellow blooms of I don't know
kissing the now warmer air.
The dogwood in bloom.
Pink outstretched.
Desperately climbing higher
to a sun too far away.
Blackhawk humming in the distance
and here it is spring,
where men stumble
one foot behind the other
in a blond confusion.
In glasses with no lenses.

In this much of me
I am sound.
Spring handed down from winter.
Reading license plates on S. 63rd
from states I've been to.
Turning corners much too fast.
Eyes to the rearview,
looking for cops.
Big and small is hard at the same time.
Broken and burning is a delicious state of becoming.
Transition is being.
From a wall of fire
to a Johnny Jump-ups purple haze.

rave little poem,
it stretches or lunges at will,
coils into a ball of tension then
springs,
snatching at something locked
bounds away laughing,
leaving the cage door open.

Jenifer Lawrence

HOME ECONOMICS

Her split ends filter sunlight
onto my jeans. In the photo,
Laura's eyes are closed,
blonde hair spread on the pillow.

She sits sideways at her desk,
says her dad took the picture
to send to this woman
who wrote the letter she holds.

In blue ink, in curves and loops
on lined paper the woman writes
about Laura's breasts as though
she has held them in her hands.

Laura folds the letter up.
She looks me in the eye.
Her skin is perfect, freckled,
her nails bitten clean.

She says while she was sleeping
her dad took off
his pajamas and snapped away.
Sometimes she wakes up

to find him on her bed.
He lays his penis between her breasts
and moves between them.
She says it is warm and slippery.

Lawrence

She says once when she opened
her mouth he pushed in. She says
it was hot and salty, that it tasted
like battery acid feels, tingly, bitter.

She could be describing a soft pretzel,
or how she learned to tie her shoes.
She pins a paper sleeve to cloth,
turns her face to the sun.

A tracing wheel lies on Laura's desk.
I pick it up, run it back and forth
along my palm, pressing in,
making red indentations.

In the background, girls are giggling.
Small motors start and stutter.
A yard of pink material lies on the floor,
pattern fastened to it, blue text

directing: *Cut here. Sew along this line.*
Pins stick out in all directions
though the teacher said be careful
to point them all one way.

I push harder, trying to feel it,
to come as close as I dare
to bleeding. The sun is warm
on my shirt. I feel the fabric

strain against my chest. *No shit,* I say,
my hands cold, the wheel digging
a dotted line that I follow
all the way back to my desk.

Lawrence

Making Out

*Six Children in a Singlewide Trailer Kissing Under
a Light Rain at the End of June*

Younger by fifteen months, I am still her older sister.
I do not tell her to move the boy's hand from her breast.
Instead I make the motion she is making with her palms
and shake my head so that she stops.

The one that's kissing her is the boy with black magnets
for eyes, lashes that curl from his lids
the way we try to curl ours, with tiny tongs
in front of the mirror. None of us know anything

about standing our ground. At our house,
the practice is to do whatever it takes to keep
the peace, less *turn your cheek* than
close your eyes and pretend.

The oldest girl is oblivious, absorbed
in the reaction of her boyfriend, pushing
her body against his, the power she wields, the boy
a spaniel whimpering at her kindness.

But my sister's breast puckers under a boy's touch
and she wants him to stop, wants me to make him.
She rubs her thighs flat-palmed, a sign
recognized but not acknowledged.

The lesson has been passed through generations
like a relay baton:
We do not save each other
because we do not know it is possible.

Lawrence

ONE HUNDRED STEPS FROM SHORE
—St. Ann's Hospital, August 13, 1971

My sister dumps puzzle pieces on the table.
We don't follow the usual rule
of not looking at the picture on the box.
Wheat bends toward the red siding of a farmhouse.
The barn is bigger than the house,
paint peels off its long boards.
A row of poplars edges the lawn
and a thicket of trees stands behind the field.

We work the puzzle, find all the edges first.
We form the frame before we begin the middle.
Mom and Dad go in and out of the waiting room.
They bring paper bowls of chocolate pudding
and little wooden paddles.

The bathroom door is heavy.
When I come out a policeman waits.
We sit on the orange couch.
Someone has drawn a daisy on it.
He asks me my name, how old I am,
asks me what I saw, how I knew.
He asks me about the pickup, where it was
on the road, where my sister was,
what I saw, what I heard.
He asks what the driver said,
a small man with white hair,
asks me what he said and I tell him.
He said he honked, he said she jumped in front of him.
He said he honked to warn her not to cross,
and she jumped in front of him.

Lawrence

The policeman asks what I saw, what I heard.
He wants to know if I heard a screech.
I tell him no, just a thud, and I ran to see
and I saw her. He asks me what I saw,
what I heard. I tell him it smelled like pennies.
I tell him I saw her and she was fine, just lying there,
hair in her eyes and a puddle beneath her head.

The policeman asks me, with his unlined notebook
and a pencil like the one I use in school.
He writes everything down, he asks me again.
He asks what I did then and I tell him.
I tell him my mother is running up the steps.
I see my mother and try to stop her,
I put my arms in front of her, tell her not to look.
She says *Let me see* and I tell her *It's Carolyn.* I tell her
it's Carolyn and that she is hit.
He asks me what then and I tell him
and he asks me what then
and I tell him.

We go back to the puzzle and we finish the house.
We build the barn and the poplar trees.
My older sister works on the wheat,
my younger sister works on the sky.
My mother sits with a puzzle piece in her hand
and peels the picture from the cardboard.
My father brings us more pudding.
He lies down on the couch and doesn't close his eyes.
We work on the puzzle and the field is full of wheat.
We start on the birch grove, the snow-white trunks.
We build the trees from the green down to wheat
and there is nothing left but sky.

Lawrence

We are holding pieces in our hands
and the waiting room door swings open.
The doctor is there in the doorway,
he stands there and puts his left palm on its window.
He stands on the threshold and doesn't come in.
His clothes are wrinkled, they are green as the walls.
His hair is silver and sticks to his forehead.
He stands in the doorway, he doesn't come in.
He sees us watching and he watches us back.

He looks at the pieces of sky in our hands
and he looks at our faces one by one.
He looks at our hands and he looks at our eyes
and he looks at my mother and no one says anything.
He takes a deep breath and says nothing.
He takes a deep breath and shakes his head.
He shakes his head from side to side
and his hair falls into his eyes.

Lawrence

THE FEEDING TIDE

Belly to palm, he taught me:
Run the double leader through the sockets.
Hooks catch and refuse to let go of the eyes.
Inside loop over the head to snub shut the mouth.

Wrap the dorsal fin. Anchor the upper hook
in the ribs, the lower just above the tail.
Place a thumbnail at the shaft, pull
without tearing flesh, snug out the slack.

Lean over the transom to rinse off the scales.
Slide the herring in to check its action,
stutter of a wounded fish in a forest of still water
on the lee shore of Marmion, trolling

in the Whaler with a four-horse Johnson,
barely moving along in the slack tide.
Strip line from the reel. Keep a thumb on the drag,
count out the depth for Kings.

For three decades, sticking to my skin:
mica moons pull me into the current.

Marty Lovins

UNTITLED

In the Gap before paved streets
rubber gun fights covered weekends
Westerns at the Roxy cost a dime
Nobody fired empty
Burt Landcaster flew with Gina
before *Playboy* revealed more
than tights and someone famous
kissing Ava Gardner's toes
Had no idea a castle existed
on 7th Ave where I would spend
more than half my life
having fun

Frank Malgesini

THE GLASS SHAPER

He draws me back, perhaps
because I am like that:

that man who
is always there
at each fair

amidst ships
and kioskos,
wishing wells

and carts
pulled by little
horses, dogs
or goats.

His small gas
torch is before
him as he moves

the glass
swizzle stick
in the flame,

the glass swooning
into motion,
drying to brittleness,

liquid flowing
through fleeting magic
into trinkets

poised to shatter across
the floors of a thousand homes.

Malgesini

THE INNER STRUCTURE

These things always come back:

not the important moments,
but a feeling associated maybe with the way
dust hung in the sunlight before you,

looking out through the barn door
when you were five years old,
when time hung in the air
like those self-same particles of dust;

or the special sweet way
the rain smelled on your grandfather's
farm over on the coast where rain

comes often
and the ground is permeated
with the sodden memory of it.

This is a different smell than the rain
at home where rain comes like a fugitive
that steals in and is gone
before you can grasp it.

The inner structure of your world
is made of such material as this;
not the information that overlays
this frame but the vague references,
fleeting impressions that form
the tangible world.

Lynn Martin

WORD

Isn't it a calling? How the mother calls her son in for supper?
How the sound of his voice calls up a thousand sighs?

How a single word—tenderness—calls forth the sea-foam green
and mustard-yellow of grandmother's quilt one slept under

as a child? Or how the wind feels on a summer's day
when its movement is irrepressible against the skin?

It's more than a scramble of letters and numbers
across a screen. It's that calling we finally answer

with the self that only begins to appear word by word—
apple—unforgettable—yellow cat—languidly—

unanswerable—Ravenna—kiss—extravagant—
alstroemeria—cloudless—green bench—celestial—

apricot—transparent—porch—reckless—cemetery—
undulant—moon—endlessly—trout—indefinable—

teeth—impenetrable—weed—incandescent—
blue plate. How each secret word opened and shone.

A rabbi once told his pupil, "When you utter a word
before God, enter that word with every one of your limbs."

I become small. I listen to be made alive. Crow chatter.
Cupboard door. Pine-wind. What is not touchable

is what touches me, the unknowable secret. I am created
by wolf cry, by rags, by fire, by salt—by that pear leaf.

Martin, L

THE NEXT STORY

Who decided how tall yellowed grass
would sway in the summer's breeze,
its hollowed self, so light-filled?

Who decided this hapless bulb
would hide the oh-so-red tulip?

If the sea could speak its name,
would it tell the secrets of tears
it holds in its wide bowl?

I wonder, sometimes, if God is ever sad?
I wonder how often the angels weep?

I wonder, too, who decides
how hard or easy it will be to die?

And what would we do without
the wind to carry us into the next story

where the moon suddenly turns
our hearts alert with its light,

where the stars tossed into constellations
haunt us with their beauty?

I don't know what I'd do
without the tenderness of old roses.

Martin, L

I don't know what I'd do
without that foolish purple finch
who sings in the windstorm.
Let us fall to our knees and kiss
the lengthening grass that never gives up,

and let our lives rise like silly pillowcases
just caught up in the wind, lifting, billowing.

Martin, L

LACE CURTAINS

This morning, how the light lifts itself,
             then falls through these lace curtains—
    is as if another world is breathing
             beyond this one
                        and I will live forever.
                 Outside the window, the apple tree
holds everything it has ever held
    within its branches. Who will see
        its radiance? House guests rise early,
    one a boy the age my child
             would have been, *ten years.*
             This could be my son.
    A truck rumbles down the hill
             between hedges of summer grasses
        and Queen Anne's lace, too tall
    to see over.
                    Why is it that anything
             lace-like, the pure look on a boy's face,
    cuts my heart into the open shape
        where what is brave must live? Who
    would have thought such fragrance
        possible from bare branches? Who
    would have thought one could rest
             one's chin on an elderberry blossom?
        Who could have known my heart, now—
             like the last November leaf,
        cut into lace in its dying—
                    would finally let the light through?

Terry Martin

IF WE COULD GO OUT TO LUNCH

We'd sit in the booth with the river view,
falls crashing over rocks as they always have,
and order salads, feeling righteous.

We'd laugh at things only the two of us share.
The woman on the bus grabbing
grandpa's new broom, thinking it was a pole.
How never saying a word,
he tried to hold it steady,
not wanting to let her down.

That time we got the giggles on the Amish tour
and couldn't stop laughing, tears pouring
down our faces, gasping and snorting
until we were sternly ushered out
into the twentieth century.

I'd tell you of the sign I saw on Old Harrah Road:
 Eat spuds.
 Be strong.
 Fear not.
How this morning, reaching into
the bathroom cabinet for my toothbrush,
I found it ribboned with toothpaste,
a small gift from my lover.

I'd show you the new silver glints in my hair.
Deeper lines crinkling my eyes
than you ever got to see.
How my hands are looking more like yours.

Martin, T

I'd ask you what you miss the most.
And we'd split a dessert—crème brulee,
maybe, roll our eyes upward, moan
at the decadence of smooth vanilla,
cool beneath its crusty golden shell.

Across the table we'd hold hands
and marvel at the fact that
your touch was my first language,
and my touch was your last.

Martin, T

MORNING CAMPFIRE

Flames lick the early air,
crackling tamarack and rising smoke
merging last night's dreams.
Hands uncurl from the cup.
Poking ashes with a stick, you rearrange logs.
Pine and coffee scent this dawn,
river rushing by as it always has
through deep canyons, cliffs scarred with age,
past weathered boulders, hunched, waiting.
At the confluence of many currents
you and I rest, released from
the thorny thicket of old habits.
Here in the rocky, dusty places
our striving means nothing.
We are learning we are not
who we thought we were.
Fingers tracing warm knuckles,
I pocket your words like small stones,
shiny and private, carry them.
I have all that I need today,
gratefully tilting my face upward
toward the warm, the changing light.

THE SECRET LANGUAGE OF WOMEN

Ironing, pressing the collar, the cuff,
sprinkling water from a pop bottle shaker,
steam hissing, spitting.
Evening up seams, each stroke
a straightening, a smoothing of features.

Trimming your bangs, Scotch Tape along forehead,
good scissors awfully close to your eyes.
Snipping, clipping across your brow,
she backs up and takes measure,
carefully cutting the even line.

Dividing, discarding, what hands know.
Holding the ripest cantaloupe,
squeezing the ready avocado,
plucking bananas and grapes
from their clustered families.

Pantry filled with mason jars—apricots, plums,
floating jewels. Lids she'll dust to a golden shine.
Pint containers lined up in the freezer.
Rows of raspberries, peaches, evenly spaced.
Storing up.

The knife's power in her hands.
Slicing the sandwich into matched triangles.
Onion diced, chopped, tiny squares sizzling
in the black iron skillet. Patting the meatloaf twice
for good luck, before sending it into the oven.

Martin, T

Each butter cookie, the same round size,
the print of her thumb pressed in.
To make sure things are even,
one sister gets to slice the cake,
but the other gets first pick.

Folding things, the care she takes.
Panties compact as they looked in the package,
socks, coupled in drawers.
Cloth napkins worn smooth,
you will press to your lips.

Feel the weight behind each simple act,
the secret language of women—
this song she's teaching you,
the song you'll learn.
And you'll know exactly what to do.

Brooke Matson

ELEMENTS

The petals of magnolias
drop their wings, throw open the shutters
to this green room.

Guest, they say,
this space is big enough for both us,
and made for neither.

If you went back to the beginning,
you'd see in a classroom
a girl reciting to herself the name *God*
so it wouldn't be swept away in the current
of all the other drifting things

she is losing and will lose.

Now, at breakfast,
three at this table
instead of two:

the girl still reciting
the poet forgetting
and deep water

lifting through the leaves.

IN THE VALLEY

It will be summer when the sun's rusty hands
rub the pickups to brass as they sleep along the highway.
From the window of a Ford, the mountains
rise ahead, overlaid by a picture of my mother
in our kitchen, peeling potatoes, skin flitting like feathers
into the sink. The topography of the land

always remains the same coming home. I land
in a wide bowl of desert I cup with my hands,
trace the rim with my thumbs, follow the unfolding feathers
of familiar thought that spread on the road: the highway
bends as we clear the ridge, descending into Mother's
hands vigorously peeling potatoes. Over the hours, the mountain

of memory will be pared to bone, as the mountains
are carved by the ice of December, when the land
is laid raw like the rumpled fur of a calf licked dry by its mother's
tongue. And with the first rain of the year, hands
tipped with red will open their palms to the sun along the highway.
Summer takes a few, leaving bones to burn, as crows leave feathers

for a child to gather, so she can build a past that feathers
back to wild horses: pintos that scaled the mountains.
These are now erased, and in their place the highway
runs down to Toppenish, a face grown creased as the land
with ritual and prayer, where Guadalupe burns inside folded
hands, inside summer shutters swung open to the heat:
    our mother

that my friend has tattooed on his back so that *Mother*
is always close. Down in the fields, the evening spreads her feathers
upon the bent bodies of the workers, their hard hands to break
the dusty earth and rake out the mountains of fruit. See how
oaks gather round the creek snaking through the dry land,
every now and then venturing close to the highway

we drive on, scales glimmering through the tall grass. Highway
soon splits into roads, to a small house where I see my mother
emerge from the doorway to meet me. Her lips land
on my cheek and her dark hair feathers my skin. I have driven
over mountains to feel her hold my face with these warm hands,
as familiar as the sound of a crow's feathered wings:
the call of mountains as their hands embrace the valley.

Matson

NEGLECTING YOUR EASEL

The consequences have been strange:
It has become harder to rise

with the morning. The gulls flock
to the banks of the river, and remain
rooted there in the rain

like white stones washed
to gray over earth's soft pages.
My easel is dry

and though I cover the portrait with a sheet,
the face hidden there unravels

in my dreams, like water
carelessly spilt.

Each morning, new cobwebs are flown
throughout the house, as if they labored
all night to sew the rooms together
where the gaps were too wide;

so I move to the kitchen and wash away
the roughness from potatoes,

and think, as I rub them, how they swelled

with the enormity of planets
in their massive turning
inside the dark room of the earth

Matson

and are unburied, whole and ready
for hands to receive—

all that was lost between
the call and response of wings.

Rita Mazur

A TREMOR OF LEAVES

—Summer 1996, Vision Problems

Along the far bank
wind lifting, or maybe
an animal breathing hard.
Lavender fog shifts slightly.
My desk is piled, layer on layer,
papers, lost bills,
forgotten tasks, phone messages.
But in this short time of vision,
only a few hours a day in focus—
I spend them on the river—
float past seventeen white pelicans
standing on slim water, reflections
mixed with single cloud puffs,
savor deep pink of sand dock—
individual bouquets
on dunes facing morning sun.

A repeat of water sounds, insistent killdeer calls,
the slap and roll of big carp, scales flashing silver;
my fingers trace every track,
move deep in deer prints,
hold each rock and Indian artifact until they shape
my hands.

Now I hold granddaughters close,
compare skin to English roses,
store the way hair changes, strand to strand.
I note every color, from cobalt of eyes
to pale pink fingernails. My daughter, their mother,
asks "Why are you staring so?"
I tell her
how beautiful they are.

David McCloskey

DEAR DAD,
—Summer, 1998

I'm standing at the kitchen sink again,
gazing out the window onto the garden
in the falling dark of yet another summer's eve,
cleaning up the Sunday dinner dishes
as we used to do so many years ago
(just Mom and me today), you know
how she scatters bowls and stuff around,
but oh! good Lord! can she still cook:
roast beef, potatoes, carrots, onions & gravy,
fresh salad and peach cobbler for dessert!

I just got back from playing golf at Laurelwood
as we used to on weekends most of the year,
shot the same score, too (some things
remain constant after 35 years!)

Mom has kept up the house and yard well—
she's a wonderful gardener as well as cook—
your rock wall is still standing firm, but
she's housebound now at 92, and
only a few of your prize dahlias survive,
though the wood violets and anemones
she bought for you have run rampant,
and your favorite geraniums ("Jack's flowers")
still blaze away on the front terrace.
And, by the way, that big Dodge you bought
just before you passed over still runs—
the one with the push-button gears
and wide-open windows—can you believe it
—it still has only 51,000 miles!

McCloskey

How's Grandma and Jim?
We miss them terribly.
Mike's OK, and about to retire from the Sierra Club,
and he and Maxine will soon return to Portland.
I married Marsha in 1966, and we live in Seattle
on the hill behind the Space Needle (remember the Fair?);
she's a quilter and writes more books than I can count.
We're carrying on the family tradition of
you and Mom as both teachers.
You've two beautiful smart grandchildren—
Amanda and Matthew—whom you've never seen,
they are gifted with your grace and wit
and you would love them dearly, as we do.

Matt recently married Anne, they're a fine couple,
and they have a new child, Katie, but we're
real concerned because Katharine Rose
is not well, though she's a fighter.

I know we've lost touch over the years, though
I feel we communicated directly for a while.
Mom asked at dinner tonight whether I ever miss you
and I went all to water, burning tears falling on my plate
(so close to the surface even now, more than half my life ago).
Ever since that damn smoke from the field burning
on "Black Friday" took your breath away,
our lives were shattered to a thousand pieces.

When you died on the Fall equinox
I was seventeen and a senior in high school, and
then when Jim was taken on the winter solstice
I feared the deep cave of grief would
swallow Mom up, but we survived somehow;
my job was to buck her up (I taught her

McCloskey

to drive when she was 59), and we
went on with our lives, though we were
never the same after our season in hell.
I think she's still kinda mad at you
for leaving so early, though I know it's only
because she wanted to grow old with you
and you with her. I used to wander
in my dreams, wondering
when you and Jimmy would ever return...

Your papers are still packed
in boxes in the closet and upstairs,
though we did bind all your articles
together and gave away copies.
But, as with my own work, no one else
seems to know what to do with it,
and we keep thinking we'll get
around to it in our own retirement.

Your brother Bob and his wife are still alive at 95,
though feeble and forgetful he still
tries to order everyone around.
Your father's sister's son, Charles Sweeney,
moved with his family to Oregon
and has been a godsend for Mom,
the only living relative left in town.
A decade ago Mom wrote up extensive genealogies
of both her Studer as well as the McCloskey family,
and distributed them to both sides.
It was a heroic labor of love and honor—
she called it "her dissertation"—but she finished it!

My friends and I went on pilgrimage to our ancestral
homeland in Ireland, and Mike did too, and we

McCloskey

both visited the rocky northwestern shores of Donegal,
where Michael McCloskey and his wife Mary
and daughter Agnes welcomed us, and
remembered the old family, and I brought home
handfuls of fragrant peat from their peat pile.

And when I visited Michael and Jane McCloskey's
unmarked gravesite in Iowa (your grandfather
and grandmother), I organized a project
among our living relatives to honor the ones
who came over and established our house in America,
and we installed a fine red granite headstone
inscribed with their names and dates,
and those of their eight children,
with twin Celtic crosses on either side,
in the old cemetery at Dubuque, and
I tried as best I could to fashion bits
and pieces into the larger story of our family.

I'm writing this message hoping for a visitation
at Linslaw County Park where we always used to stop
on our way to the coast—remember the green
reflecting pools in the scoured rock steps
of the Siuslaw River, with the deep forest overhanging
and life gliding sweetly by? And I want you to know
that the mountains and forests and rivers and
the pounding ocean are still here, all
the beauty & power & tragedy
that is Oregon perdures.
Oregon is still here!

In my own life I've explored outwards
from our old house on Villard street
layer by layer, until I fell under the spell

McCloskey

of the whole Pacific Northwest region
we now call "Cascadia," a land of falling waters,
mountains and rivers, sea and sky, without end,
my greater home, our new heartland.

And I've tried to listen to its muse,
and love poetry and literature as you did
and your father before you, and learn
to sing the song the land gives us.

I'm finishing this letter I've been
writing you but don't know how to send
standing on top of Cape Perpetua
overlooking the vast Pacific, shining salmon waters,
where you can reach out and touch the far horizon,
feel the curved rolling edge of the world
carrying us forward into another day...

Mom says hello, and thinks of you often, lovingly,
and looks forward to seeing you soon.
Please remember us to all the others
we've known and those unknown
but whom we still depend upon.
Say a special prayer for our little Katie, and
watch out for her if she comes over to your side!

                                    Much love,
                                    your David

ing to the west
ummit peaks white
clouds.

en on Summitview,
uth window ledge
e theory of composition
es, "All I want to do is l
taking place somewhere/
wn./I love that./
tiful facts/
is taking place./
he language
The stuff
anguage."

Kevin Miller

THIS MORNING AT THE POLE

a line greets you, unafraid,
it says, hello, *Hello*.
It needs you more than you
know, it needs you for life,
you bring breath to a line
otherwise flat black on white.
You make this mouth to mouth
and when you hold the faces
you know behind your eyes,
it thumps this poem on the chest
and starts the heart which is your
heart, and your heart gives
this place on this pole a chance
at life, the ability to move.
That Beauty Bush
by the corner of the house
becomes what it's called
only after we look and say *Yes*.

Miller

MAN, RIVER, OCTOBER

He takes two photos, the bridge over the Yakima River
with two men and without. The light holds time,
fall, and the dry trail to Snoqualmie. One man
in the photo shows his wife, she says *No one sees
the world the way he does.* The photos prove her
wrong, they make his view their view, the men
gone offers them an answer. They cross low water
see through *next* and *when.* Wind scatters faces
and voices each carried close. October without rain
whirls what has been again, what remains caught
in color will fail in a succession of etched limbs.
The photo without men is a one man shot, it says
what all three know—the way it was and will be.

POEM IN HONOR OF JUDITH SKILLMAN'S READING AND THE REPUBLICAN CONVENTION, 1996

After a good rain, goldfinch string
their music through the service berry trees.
My wife thinks she's Saint Francis.
She charms the cedar wax wing
which lights close enough to touch.
She tells me Francis' theory of containers,
take from the full, fill the empty.
This works for her, the music of birds,
a song from St. Francis, and all those nests
the shape of cupped hands waiting.

James Milliron

SILVES

The Moors liked this place.
They stayed awhile—400 years.

The ramparts of Castelo dos Mouros
are well defined muscles, chiseled from
red sandstone, hiding dungeon chambers
and labyrinthine tunnels.

Delicious like the oranges
south of Silves; poets, orators
and historians ruled until
their time was up saith
the crusading knights of Santiago.

Eleven centuries have humbled
these hilltop walls. Its cistern died
of thirst. Below the fortress, well
fed sheep graze as quietly as
the buried religious secrets.

The castle and holy cathedral
are little compared to the freedom of
music found on the rough cobblestone
steps, downward at Cafe Inglais on our
Lord's Day.

The smiling guitarist is a long way
from Ecuador. The seductive voice is
traditional Bossa Nova and she
passionately chronicles Brazil's
lyrical colonization of Portugal.

Susan Moon

SURVIVAL

A locust tree will do anything to live:
crown its thorns with blossoms so profuse
birds will trip and bees will swoon.
Make a compromise with its skeleton,
send out suckers across the road
or in the garden.
          And the leaves?
Yes, they are green, but small
and arranged like hands with oval fingers,
seven sets along a cartilage of stem.
They are the skin, no,
    they are the veins, no,
        they are the vessels.
              No.
They are the temples
where light is stored.

Tom Moore

She Became Her Mother, the Poem Not Written But Held Close to Heart, Two and a Half Years Later

Cool Sunday afternoon
children watching Disney
she walks in with her father.
In her hands she has a bowl of
potato salad; it is made with
mayonnaise and Miracle Whip
"like mom," she says.

At the mention of potato salad
I look over to her, standing by
the counter in Sue and Gary's kitchen.
In her sunglasses, I catch her
right profile and see her mother.
The chin and bone structure,
the hair and lips, straight-backed,
her mother's daughter, and I turn from
memories and the scene.

The Mariners on T.V. that Sunday
morning Betty began her struggle,
my broken promise that she would
be out in no time.
Nobody goes to the hospital
once and never returns. No one does.
Then I as outsider, new to family
I could only watch and pray.
It just couldn't happen.
Lisa and Gayla, Gary too, there with
her. I on the fringe waiting and watching.

Moore

I remembered the last meal:
pot roast with carrots
and potatoes, tossed salad,
rolls, potato salad,
and lemon meringue pie.
At the end I remember thinking I wish
I had known that was the last dinner.
It would have meant more. I could have told
her how much I appreciated her.
I could have told her how much I loved
her cooking.

Moore

LISTS

Tom Moore wrote lists. He wrote them
in a tight legible hand. The language
was minimal, no wasted words. He
learned this as an engineering student
at Texas A&M. Navy flight school honed
this skill even more. All those pre-flight lists.
Checking for water in the fuel and
determining that the controls had free and
full travel. Once the aircraft was fired up
he would wait until engine temperature
gauge moved from red to the green.
Only then would he roll out.
Later he wrote lists for his son and daughter.
Instructions on how to start the boat or check
the boiler at the shop in winter.
Everything was there, each detail
clear, clean, accessible, simple.

THE LAST LOAD

It begins with the sharp words
in the kitchen, the pressure of death
translated to two sore backs and the
too tired couple. The winter chill of morning
sets the mood for the last of runs.
She sits against the passenger window and
studies the skiff of snow on the broken sidewalk
of their block. Her breath soon fogs the glass,
yet she stares. He steers the big Ford seeing
nothing but the lifting left to do. The Sunday morning
traffic is light as most people are home reading the
Herald or getting ready for church. No mass for these two.
They're stuck on the wrong ends of heavy objects.

Crossing 16th Avenue he notices a man walking
down Tieton Drive with a dog. The walker holds
the leash with both hands. As he accelerates towards
the museum, he sees the man is wearing dark glasses
and a stocking hat. His hands are gloved and as
they pass, the dog walker makes a slight correction
with the hand closest to the dog's collar.
Neither he nor the dog break stride.

At that moment, unknown to the walker, the driver
recognizes man and dog. He has known him for
30 years and they have been friends for 25.
It is warmer in the cab, he notices his
wife, and he is filled with joy. That moment,

the dead father is forgotten, icy words melt, and his back
doesn't hurt. At the end of Franklin Park,
he looks back, sees his friend walking away
through the blowing snow, and says,
"Lisa, that was Jim Bodeen walking his dog."
Although she says nothing in return or turns to
look herself, he knows she heard him.

Keely Murphy

ANGELS

I am painting angels. These are spray painted.
Street angels. Independently, Blayne writes about
how they steal lipstick from the dead
and draw on each others' bodies.
These are my angels, angels who smoke cigarettes,
wear denim and heels, they are urban.
They are sweet talkers.
They have five o'clock shadow,
they watch over me, like a film, feet up on the chairs, being
shushed by the theater attendants—
talking, spilling coins and candy all over the place.
These angels have gum stuck on the bottom of their shoes,
they pray like cat calls,
summoning up like street bandits,
selling shit for cheap, hands in pockets,
hair loose and tangled from walking outside.
They have tongues that taste like brick and mortar,
they are sweet eyed and mischievous.
These are angels with agendas and appetites.
These are my angels.
They will throw it all away for anything.
They watch me sleep and smear my dreams and
whisper secrets in my ears and they
push each other out of the way,
they smack their gum, they
zip their coats and slam doors.
These are my angels, desperate creative things,
nonchalant— zealous.
Gray winged sidewalk sweeping metropolis citizens,
weaving in and out, drawing on the alleys with sharpies,
leaving messages in bathroom stalls,

Murphy

sneaking into bars, drowning in decibels,
screaming at night,
humming down aisles buying toothpaste in the day,
pretty hipped angels.
They hold your hand like a first date,
put sticks of gum in your pocket,
knock on doors softly, lean in—like sluts,
write you poems you'll never hear.
They love you like that.

Murphy

To You, Julia

This is to you great grandmother,
and your Duncan Fife table,
that I am about to give away to a stranger
as an antique, for not even cash in exchange.
I'm giving away a piece of you soon, because
I don't have space for it any more and it is broken
and I wish I could keep it and love it like I should
but my mother isn't sorry about it leaving us,
and I felt that you should know that I am a little sorry,
and you should know that I am keeping the chairs
that go with it, because those are my chairs and your chairs
and I wish I didn't feel like I was giving away
thousands of dinners you cooked, but I do.
And I wish I didn't feel like I am devaluing
family heirlooms, or just plain family, but I do.
So, you should know that I am glad that you cooked
those dinners, and sorry I didn't know you,
sorry I'm giving away a piece of you to a stranger,
but, know that I realize the loss,
and that I will do it begrudgingly.
Thank you for the table you didn't know I would have some day.
The one you didn't know I would give away, too.
And, I still have the vanity, the one my dad repainted,
because you got it pretty beat up, and left cigarettes
burning on it all the time, and my mother said
that you were a funny lady, that they all sort of rolled their eyes
when you would come to visit, that you would make
lemon meringue and sling the batter all over the living room
as you walked about the house, beating it.

Murphy

I wish you were to here to tell me to
"Just, get rid of the old thing."
So, let's say that you would, let's say that you would sit with me
at my new table, it has only two chairs, and we would sit
across from each other and you might hold my forearms for a
minute and tell me what you know, what you feel I need to know
and I would look into your clear pale eyes and say, "Of course."
So, let's say that you are still with me.

Murphy

DISTILLED

I want to tape leaves to my eyelids
have all the oranges and reds block out
and let in only their light
I want them over my mouth and ears
so that all of it is beautiful—
all of it speaks of autumn, and change—
so I can live unplagued by my own eyes
and ears, so that I can't speak unless
it is crimson, fading chlorophyll.
I don't want anything but orange and red for
the next few weeks, don't give me normal daylight
or dusk without these filters
I don't trust this transition inside me
I get unexplainably sad
I lay down early and sleep
like I'm walking off a pull in my leg
I need to cleanse out the summer
get distilled in this season, get an equal
concentration of remembering and leaving.
Let's put paint on everything,
pour it down the sides of buildings,
make rivers in the streets,
it will all be deep orange, red the color of muscle,
and we'll rake our yards and mix it in
and then I will make a monument
for everything I've ever believed—
in a sculpture, and we'll put it downtown.
We'll raise our hands and then I'll be able to move on
I'll know where to go from here
I will trust my heart murmur
and I will be full of autumn and October
it will pour out of my mouth
and we'll go on from here.

German Nava

HARD WORKING

Cars
broken
down
beside the road.

Kids
waiting
in the house
to be loved.

Juan Ortega

BREAKPOINT

How I want the bullshit to end.
How I need it to end.

Is it Satan or human society?
Which is worse? Should I care?

Give me the capability to make everyone see
what I see—
majestic landfills and ominous clouds
of carbon monoxide.
Beauty on earth becomes real estate.
Countrysides become paved roads.
"Hey NASA is life on this planet
not God enough?"

We are all responsible for this.
The earth gives until it can no longer
and one day…one day it too will die.

Jorge Padilla

FOR ZACH

Hanging with the homeboys
whistling at Ruccas
trying not to get shot
I wonder if there's no place for a thug,
if there's heaven for a gangster.
I wonder if I can give my mom a hug.
Before I go I want to thank her.

Gail Pearlman

NEW YEAR'S PROMISES

I am a teacher and a lover
of wild places,
and I make these promises to my students:
I insist that you always see the face,
the strained sweat on the chin of the boy
crossing the border in a boxcar,
the confusion in the eyes of the caribou
approaching the pipeline with her calf,
the trapped terror of the car thief
about to be raped in his cell,
the 16-year-old
handcuffed while registering,
his stricken mother pleading with the guard.
I insist that you risk
seeing these faces, no matter where
they insist you go.

This is a lot to risk. I have no maps
for where you're going. And there's more.
For I am a lover of wild places, places that hold
the untamed parts of our hearts, yours and mine.
I ask you to look until you see—
the fragile lichen
clinging to an Arctic hillside,
the glint of thin sun on a grizzly's blond coat,
caribou rollicking over the tussocks,
a wolf, regal and distant, tracking the herd,
razored peaks silhouetted in blazing pink
at 2 a.m., the clear water of the Nigu
pummeling down the valley floor, a relentless
searing sun on the treeless tundra,

hundreds and hundreds of unbroken miles,
miles and lives we haven't yet slashed to pieces.
I ask you to think about what loss means,
why everything depends
on our saving these places, places that hold
the untamed parts of our hearts, yours and mine.

I have no maps for where you're going.
I ask you to think on these things.
The thought police
have been pounding us. We hear the words,
new words, or old words redefined,
patriot, homeland security, axis of evil, terrorism,
enemy combatant, collateral damage, alien,
but I insist that you ask what is behind those words.
What if a patriot is someone who fights
against thought police and unjust wars,
what if homeland security is love and compassion,
what if the axis of evil is domination and greed,
what if terrorism is winter and no food, illness and no medicine,
what if an enemy combatant is someone who torches the fields
and holds the patent on the medicine,
what if collateral damage
is the torn and bloodied face of a child?
And what if there is no such thing
as an alien?

The thought police
have been pounding us,
and we have no maps, but I ask you
to break out of prison, run like hell,
don't stop until you find the truth.

Pearlman

I promise I will ask this. And I promise
I will not succumb to fear
I will not succumb to fear
I will not succumb to fear.

January, 2003

José Pete

Mom

You sheltered all eight.
You fed us.
You even took care of us when things got bad.
When I came home crying, you would always find a way to
make me happy.

But now you can't do that.
Now you are in heaven.
Now you are taken care of by God.

I see signs of you trying to tell me things.
I see you here and there.
But only if I could hold you one more time.

But I gotta stay strong
and become the man you wanted to raise me to be.
But it was your time and there was nothing I could do.
I still love you, Mom.

Dan Peters

from IN THE EASEMENT OF ABSENT TIES

The night before we take off,
they haven't seen anything.
We all light up.

Earlier at dinner, as cold torpedoes arrived on trays,
Marcus told the table about a Korean tradition.
He said you can't pour your own beer.
It's customary to fill your neighbor's glass.
A nearly perfect ritual.
We added, if you're empty,
it's acceptible to bump a friend and ask for a little help.

• • •

Rob,
     Are you with me?
     My class is learning about stories.
     I would like to tell them,
     unexplainable things—sometimes awful shit—
     will happen.
     We don't expect it but it still happens.
     It makes what we know come apart.

     In our book, Kittredge says stories are important
     because they help us make sense,
     even temporarily, of the world.
     He calls it coherency. I'm not so sure.
     Stories help us live.
     Even when we find them out of control.
     They say we're not the first—may not be the last.
     By guiding us outward, they put us together.

Peters

This is a story about going away.
It doesn't have to make sense.

I can't write any more until I write this part.

Ten years ago I was in an accident.
I caused it.
An accident.
Late afternoon. Summer.
My mom asked me to take her down to pick up her car.
On my way home,
a small boy ran in front of me and was killed.
There's a lot more to the actual story of that day,
but these are the basic facts.
He was three.
I was eighteen.
When I stopped and threw open the door,
the air smelled like rubber.
He was running to join friends on the other side of the street.
I was barefoot.
His name was Roberto Gonzales.
The pavement was hot.
His mother, I think, came screaming out of a white duplex,
lifted his head off the road
and cradled him in her lap.
I got out of the car,
sat on someone's lawn
and pulled grass up in my fists.
He died at the hospital.
He would be the same age as a seventh grader at Wilson.
It was in the paper. It is one of my secrets.
We sold the car I was driving.
Everyone feels sorry, somehow.
There's a nail pounded in the pavement where my tires caught.

Peters

So. This trip with you, and the hike afterward,
hoping to get things straight, ten years later.
I thought I'd finally had enough.
I wanted to make it stick.
Big me.
I make the same mistakes in this poem.
The next stretch is a blur.

• • •

Rob,

    When I walked the Iron Horse Trail
    below the headwaters of the Yakima
    I couldn't see my shadow until I stepped into Tunnel 49.
    Once I did, it was there before me.
    The archway narrowed the dim sun.
    One third into the tunnel, the sun disappeared.
    No draft pulled me forward.
    The light bent at the other end.
    It cast my shadow over the river-rock.
    My eyes never adjusted to everything black
    in the easement of absent ties.

    Here is the best I can do:
    Stories have power.
    They are locations and instructions.
    They change each time you move.
    And you have to move.

I took the day off on the tenth anniversary of the accident.

Peters

I typed up all of my journal entries for that date,
then went outside and sat in the park across from our lot.
The house next to ours burned down earlier that summer
and was torn apart.
The foundation was coming out.
We lived so close, a lilac tree touched both houses.
One side of it burned.
We weren't home when it happened.
I still can't see how our place didn't go up.
While I rested on the curb across from the two houses,
I thought about how we were spared.
Looking down, I noticed blue glass
sown like islands on the blacktop near my feet.
I picked up a few of the pieces and inspected them.
I found a sticker on one.
A bottle of Gravity cologne, splintered by a high school kid.
Some shards had painted letters.
White capital A on one and on another, IT, from the full name.
The balance of the word, too scattered to recover.

LETTER TO STUDENTS WHO ARE NOT HERE

—In memory of Karen, Jessica and Jason,
fighting a fire, on a mission

Words and books
Like a small creek off a high ledge
Gone in the dry air.
        —Gary Snyder, "Piute Creek"

The hills are green and will be for as long as a month.
Then, as the cheatgrass matures, they will turn red.
By the time you come home,
fewer than before,
they will have changed to various shades of brown.
Now, though, they are green and some mornings,
when clouds cover the valley, you can squint your eyes
and almost believe you are in another country
where all year long, the hills remain as round and bright
as these ridges are today.

Not quite a year ago, I wrote another letter.
I said *I don't have anything other than easy answers*
that seem tired before I can get them out of my mouth.
Much later, I saw things were passing through me.
You could call it grief or maybe it was just so much had changed.
My friend, who was my high school teacher,
drove me around for more than an hour.
He said, *I went to landscape.*
He copied down this line: *No one loves rock, yet here we are.*

Beginning with Murray's letter before Christmas,
old words have come back to me in new ways.
I didn't know what to do with this, either.

Peters

Then it happened five times in five months—
Bales and Hiler and Matson and Lohrasbi and
two days ago, another friend, a long distance runner,
brought down what was left of my resistance.

Outside my window the sound of a lawnmower
drifts back and forth.
I am not where I was, and you are not here, any more.
The ridges change as they did before any of this happened—
before we lost so much.
That's no kind of answer, but I will stand by it.

Across the valley, I can see pillars of smoke where orchards stood.
The trees behind your high school
empty of blossoms in the wind and rain.
Meanwhile, those beside the river continue to fill with leaves.

BIRD IN MY HAND

I woke up at 6:30, an hour before the sunrise.
I felt my chest tighten with the cold I couldn't shake.
When I coughed, I saw spots.
I drank two doses of expired Robitussin
and went to read about the Mariners online.
In about ten minutes, while it was still dark, I felt different.
I walked to the bathroom, knelt down and waited.
After I got sick, I let both cats out and curled up on the couch.
An hour after dawn, I woke again.
I walked into the kitchen where I saw our cats
sitting on the window sill.
One of them, probably Ester, brought a bird.
She has never done this.
I let them in and grabbed a grocery bag.
The body rolled easily off the sill.
Its weight barely pulled on the plastic.
I placed the bird in the trash, came inside and saw your mom,
still carrying you.
I said nothing of the omens I'd seen and felt.

On the way to the hospital we talked about payday.
We decided to use the checkbook.
We promised to love you as much as we love each other.
At 10 to 10 we pulled into Memorial and by 11:30,
you were here.
That night, we read to you, played Greg Brown for you.
The next morning, I drove home and sent pictures of you
out into the world.
I was on my way back to the hospital
at the start of your second twenty-four hours.

Peters

Waiting for a light at the corner of Summitview and 16th,
I happened to look to my left and saw a boy in a little yellow bus
chewing on his coat collar and waving at me.
He picked me out for some reason
and was twisted around in his seat, staring.
For a moment I wondered why he was on this bus.
Was there something wrong with the boy?
Was there something special about this child?
Below his smiling face, the word EPIC.
I raised my arm and waved as he pulled away.
My hand, a wing above the wheel.

SKUNK IN THE WELL

I'd come to believe that this child made me even.
I saw her whiteness as my own.
Then one morning, at the end of our first summer together—
long walks through the neighborhood, neighbors smiling,
me smiling back—
a father and his son arrive at my door
and place a trap in my window well.

The skunk dropped in overnight.
I watched its muddied tail
sweep across the small basement window
while my child slept upstairs.
So I went to the book and I called the man.
He said, *Sit tight.* I did just that.
Through the monitor, I heard Ella stir in her crib.
The animal paced around, sniffed the air,
searched my bright basement with its black eyes.

That morning as Ella and I played on the floor
I listened to the animal grow desperate.
I could hear it claw the glass.
It tried to tunnel out.
A hole formed at the top of the concrete half-circle.
When I went outside and looked down the well, it was gone—
curled up asleep or burrowing deeper into the soft ground.

Within minutes, a truck backed into our driveway.
The man was fit, clean, compact and handsome.
Blond, close-cut hair and mustache.
He smiled and shook my hand.
His teenage son rolled out wearing a black concert shirt.
The father took a long knife from his truck

and asked where it was.
The three of us walked around back, Ella in my arms.
He stood over the well,
then knelt beside it.
He set the knife on the ground
and braced himself before bending half his body into the hole.
I can't see 'im, he said when he emerged.
He went back to the truck for a cage and a tin of cat food.
He leaned in again and set the trap.
It'll get hungry, he said when he surfaced. *Call me when it hits.*

The cage lay empty all day and night. No movement. No sign.
In the morning, the skunk was in the trap.
Ella was not yet up.
I made the call.

The father and son returned.
We cleared a path from the backyard to his truck.
The father said, *Why don't we settle up before I get 'im outta there?*
Whatever he said, I paid.
He took a small blue tarp from his cab and cut a slit in the center.
The father put on rubber gloves
and reached the tarp into the well.
We were still and silent.
He drew his arm out, the handle of the cage
held through the slit in the tarp.
Not yet knowing what was next, not having asked,
I looked at them out of the side of my eye.
The scene was tender.
He tucked the blue plastic around the cage with great care.
He was gentle because he had to be.
We looked at the cage and at each other.

He folded and closed the tarp
with thin white masking tape as if it were a gift.
He worked quickly.
The son waved and climbed back into the cab.

Without prompting, the father took off his gloves,
walked over to me and shook my hand.
We whispered a few words back and forth—thanks, mainly—
and the three of them drove away.

Inside, the house vibrated differently.
I should feel absolved. Should feel free.
But I feel the presence of the skunk.
I try to imagine how it fell in the first place.
I wonder what it did all day,
dug deep in the cool earth beneath my house.
Alone again with my daughter, I question its fate.

Three days after the father and son left with the skunk,
a tattered peacock feather comes to rest on the lip of the well.
A week after that, another skunk, this one smaller, a child,
falls in the same place at the same time.
Before I can panic, the young skunk leaps out
and disappears so swiftly that I question if it was ever there.
I am left to wait for the next thing to drop in the well.
It may be that I am meant to attract
snakes and mice and young skunks to our door,
that what came before is not forgiven
but returns, juvenile, potent.

Linda Pier

THE SAGE OF HOME

It's the first of May.
Again I read your manuscript
and my notes.
For "Kilometer Zero" I write
"the sage of home."
Early this evening I retrace
the familiar route up the canyon.
The sage is still "dusty green like
olive trees washed in rosy light."

Stopping at a favorite pull-out
I check the hatch—caddis are emerging.
You taught me how to read the water.
I look for rises in feeding lanes
and see a patterned dimpling here and there.
I look west as the sun slips
behind the curves of overlapping hills.
I bend down and smell the pungent sage.
Today I hope to catch not trout
but you and me and our time
together on the River.

Tom Pier

THE MAN WHO FISHED TOO MUCH

We are scarce our fathers' shadows cast at noon.
        —John Donne

At Ketchum when he auctioned off Papa's rod,
he was all redemption and regret:
"I once fished two hundred days in a row."
Then he was more Hemingway-handsome than Papa,
but still the chunky child of Paris,
the Mr. Bumby of *A Moveable Feast*
and the photo by Man Ray, a babe in his father's arms.
Later Jack fished fine and far off on the spring creek
where Papa once shot ducks
with the shotgun that was soon to kill him.
How many times he must have thought of his father's work
and then his own confession written between war
and fishing trips, a life of misadventures, he called it:
how it was to be beautiful and blessed skiing with "Coop"
in the Sawtooths, teaching French in Idaho
bringing Spain and Shakespeare and Company
to the Mountain West, having adorable daughters.
Beside Papa's memorial on the Big Wood
the aspens still shake to think of it.
How cursed it is to love the surface of the earth
and find the art to render this so well.
Then you come to know your kin must live
in the shadow of these same trees,
beatific while they wait for you and other
Hemingways to die, too many at their own hands.

DOWN TO THE COTTONWOOD BOTTOMS

They call the place Parachute:
three converging mesas form an angle
like those of a chute and its cords descending to the valley.
And a softer fall it must seem to Fred who's escaped
the dark mountain heights upriver,
a terrain of booze and heartbreak,
to this high plateau, itself a freak of demographics.
When shale oil went bust, the mesa became cheap housing,
out of range of celebrity slope and condominium,
way too down valley for all
but the very weary and the out of luck.
The fierce red and green hills upriver give way
to gentler gray buttes, and the valley
opens up to cottonwood bottoms.

It was Fred's way to slip away in the night,
after the wedding, after the funeral.
Next morning we'd know there'd been bourbon
in the coffee, vodka in the iced tea.
With or without the kids, with or without the wife,
he'd be gone.
The sweet voice we hear on the radio
reminds Fred of his wife's; together we hear them cry:
"I'll never get over those blue eyes. I see them everywhere."

Now at night I slip into Parachute; saving him I save myself.
When I head for home, I leave him harnessed in:
"This is a good place to dry out," he says to me,
and I'm bound to agree, thinking a brother could do worse
than be born again in a place like this
where the deer are as common as young people
and wilder than they in a land of retirement and refuge.

Pier, T

On the Way to Salpetrière

When the Princess died on the way to Salpetrière,
the network news didn't tell you Foucault
had died there too, or how—of AIDS—or that Freud
had studied there, that Pinel and Charcot had begun
their dark probings there or that long before any of them
France, looking for light,
had buried centuries of darkness there.

These grand old stones tell a story: it's a history
of how a culture treats the latest version of its ill,
an unheard opera in the theater of pain.

I think of de Sade at Charenton and know I've heard
two stories: one about his being here and one about his not:
I don't know which to believe. It's all too easy to imagine.
Certainly the mad were here and the merely poor.
Many taken from the street or the road were here—
vagabonds and ladies of the evening, many Manon Lescauts
soon off to the New World, like convicts.
Men of a new science charted the history of hysteria here,
case after case, readying for Vienna,
nervously exploring fresh wounds.

From our café on St. Marcel we regard
the modern glass which conceals the ancient home
of great doctors, dark science, and celebrity death.
At lunch, staff from the ancient place find their way
to our restaurant. We eavesdrop and try to fold ourselves
into the deep layers of pain.

Pier, T

Electroshock and scalpel seemed to follow them here.
There's a riot of traffic on the Boulevard of the Hospital:
France is scandalized over bad blood.

I recall the afternoon we stepped across the boulevard
and like ghouls wandered among the grounds,
strolling from glorious arcade to flowered lawn,
trying to resist the screams that still echoed down the halls.
Beneath the octagonal dome we remembered rumors
of a museum of horrors, as secret as the Vatican's,
but what we imagined was dark enough and cruel.
Even now from Paris I think I hear the klaxons cry.

Timothy Pilgrim

Hear No Evil

Montana campfire. Cabin buried by night sky.
My father's past carved 50 years
around eyes gone half-blind.
Finally he lets slip
one piece of a camouflaged life.
South Pacific, New Guinea,
second world war, Army directive:
Turn Japanese back here,

now, for good, or watch them swarm
Australia's beaches, Rising Sun
matching Coral Sea wave for wave.
There, then, desperate men
give war a new face. Obey orders to pay natives
two dollars silver for each enemy head.
Dad, back from regular killing, for rest,
for good, undertakes a new mission.

Bury their skulls, some on bamboo stakes,
others piled about the camp.
Carry them sleepy, two at a time, smiling.
Fill trenches-turned-graves. Fling others
into caves with decaying comrades
frozen in battle crouch, licked to death
by flames thrown in like afterthoughts.
Shovels cover memories deep in loam.

GIs, Dad, welcome new orders —EARS ONLY—
but this exacts a fresh toll. Husbands
snip orchids listening to moonlight
from dozing children and wives. A generation

Pilgrim

will hear no evil, detect no lies.
Dad finds it easy to slip off to sleep.
I drink sake all night.
Fend off my dreams with a carving knife.

...ird, one motion, har...

...s the squall line passes
...e tosses the flowers bac...
...side the light jacket for t...
...hirt pocket. He takes his...
...he light blue lines sha...
...e stands alone with the...
...vice looking across the...
...eeing the line of green...
...e shore and
...alizes "everywhere wa...

...om Moore
...0

Charles Potts

HIDE

I am a boy again,
Riding shotgun in a black and red
1948 Dodge pickup with my dad,
Crossing the Arco desert
With our cargo of cured hides.

My father was a government trapper
And I'm a government trapper's son.
Halfway to the hidehouse on
Yellowstone Avenue in Idaho Falls,
We plow through an Atomic Energy Commission plot.

The mink, the muskrat and the coyotes,
To say nothing of the beaver,
Have turned themselves inside out
Into Levi's I might get to wear,
Clean new clothes to school
With the animals under my skin.

Potts

HARROWING

Harrows are dragged behind tractors across fields
Hydraulically or under their own weight in gravity
Breaking up clods after plowing to level the field
For seeds that grow into plants that feed us all.

Around and around or back and forth heavy disks
Lighter springtoothed and spiketoothed harrows
Raise topsoil to the level of dust and aggravation
When the wind blows it down your neck and into your teeth.

Tractors are slow, time is taken off the farmer's
Allotted skein to be burned up by children who think
Bread grows in plastic bags on supermarket shelves
Under florescent lights beyond automatic doors in air
    conditioned air.

Who cares for the land now that soil has been turned into
Dirt by petro-chemical agribiz as it hydroponically sprouts
Genetically altered seeds into super crops in silicate soil
With all the humus and consistency of pulverized glass.

Harrow the land, harrow the poem
Drag it back and forth in front of the audience
Until some of the teeth sink in.

Marjorie Power

To Tishku, Hovering

Why do you follow me?
I don't know where I'm going.
Besides, this morning I need space
to watch dew disappear from rose petals.
Shouldn't you be at work, launching the sun?
Why rivet your gaze wherever I cast mine?
If I glance at a glass of lemonade
you grab the pitcher and guzzle.
I pluck a grape or two, and you
horse down what's left of the bunch.
As though I, not you, had created the earth.
As though you were one of *my* creatures,
a much regretted mistake—or a shadow
whose counterpart I neglected
to pull from the clay.
Speaking of shadows, Tishku,
mine has taken a lover. So move.

Rob Prout

1973

I returned to the U.S. from Hong Kong
with Julie and another couple, Hank and Sue.

We had taught together for three years
and were ready to change education.

We traveled through the West
and landed in Yakima, Washington.

Julie's brother was pastor at Mt. Olive Lutheran Church
out on Tieton Drive.

The church had recently built a new house,
leaving an old orchard house that had been the first parsonage.

We four approached the congregation with a plan to start
an elementary school using the old house
as our home and classrooms.

We offered to teach and administer the new school
in return for our room and board.

The congregation met and considered our offer.

A month later we watched the West Valley Volunteer Fire Dept.
raze the old house as a practice session,
and as a favor to the congregation.

There was a bare ballfield on that spot for a few years.

Maybe somebody learned to hit or pitch or catch there.

I went to Central for a Master's Degree in Education.

Omar Ramírez Cruz

FAREWELL

I am leaving now
and there is no return

The memories leave with me
My thoughts stay with you

Those times that we have shared together are unforgettable
They were happy times and sad times

I have learned how to see your world
You have taught me how to continue with my life

I will miss the place where you used to sit
leaving behind my heart with you

Understanding your person was not easy
I thank God that he put your beauty by me

I am still scared to continue my life without you
but it is time for me to leave

Thanks for letting me be part of your world
even though you were above me

I am sure that you will find *felicidad*
I wish you the best

I will never forget you, hoping to never see you again
This place will always be in my heart like the thorn you left
    inside of me

I had illusions
Now they have left

Bill Ransom

Doble Tracción

Sunday afternoon, we're in the old Lada, Adán's driving.
I squeeze in the back with the kids. We're heading for Somoza's
private lake for a dip. I don't know how to say "four-wheel drive"
and we need one tomorrow to get in and out of the mountains.
My pocket dictionary only gives me what I already know:
"four" and "wheel" and "to drive." Yolanda slips me
that look I got the time I announced I was pregnant and
meant embarrassed. "A truck that drives with all wheels
of force," I say, and everyone laughs. "Claro," Yolanda says.
"Es 'doble tracción'." The kids test my pronunciation.
Test again. We talk, then, about how to borrow a doble tracción
for tomorrow. We'll have to lie—the roads up north are mined,
and good trucks, hard to come by. We pass an old man driving
a mule cart full of shell casings. "¡Mira, Bill!" Angelina says. She
leans across me to point at the mule. "¡Doble tracción!"

Jean Richardson

TOMB RAIDER (WITH ANGELINA JOLIE IN MIND)
Talking about love is like dancing about architecture.
—Playing by Heart

I have seen it three,
maybe five times, now.
That first hot Saturday
I sat in the darkened theater
gnawing my eager heart
with excitement.

Last time
I took my teenage niece.
"Sit. Watch," I said.
Know this is all possible—
the bungy jumping to classical music,
the black leather and self-assurance,
the parachuting in a Jeep
into the jungle to save the world,
never doubting that you can.

You can.

This is as possible for you
as Willis, Stallone, and Heston are
for the boy at the next desk.
Like Gina Davis,
you can be a hired assassin
or ride triumphantly over a cliff.
You choose.

You choose,
and I am right behind you.

Richardson

You choose,
and when it's time to count the cost,
I will count it with you.
There will be costs.
There always are.
For all of us.

We need our heroes.
We need women who are whole,
blood and guts intact,
to show us the way,

not sweetened, skirted,
submissive bits of treacle.
That way lies poorly paid
prostitution.
That way lies
a mind caught in a hobble skirt,
a future thrown off balance
by high heels.

If I can give you
just one thing
let it be this theater-darkened afternoon
to take away
put under your pillow
and soak into your dreams.
You will need it,
I am sure,
when "they" close in
tempting you with short skirts,
high heels,
and soul-searing grins.

Ann Reierson

NIGHT TIME ANXIETY

It usually arrives
right at that moment

when awake is asleep
or asleep is awake

I don't know which.

It hits hard-urgent but I don't know
what It is. It is very important.

Something I've forgotten to do.
Something that must be done.

Like setting a burglar alarm.
We don't have a burglar alarm.

While I am in the sleepy state
I think I know what It is.

I assure myself that It is OK.

Then I arrive in the awake state
and It is unknown again.

Tim Reierson

Our Love

Our love is a toaster,
with pale toast, burning pains and smoke.
We have lived and adjusted
to the warm golden brown we can depend on.

Our love is a compost pile,
hiding burning heat deep within,
refining kitchen scraps into beautiful soil.

Our love is Hertha's yard,
where weeds grow to maturity in jungle beds
along with flowers.
Little birds sing from the heart, swinging from our donated
sunflowers.

I will sing of the toaster and the compost,
I will raise a glass to Hertha.
An honest way to live as one is our prayer and praise, my love.

Corey Demetrius Robinson a.k.a. Mr. Adversary (A.D.V.)

A.D.V.

They call me Mr. Adversary cause I'm a very
adverse person adversity may describe my life
but not my purpose my service has been
adverted to advertising the streets and all of my
advertisements are physically discreet advance
from the advice of an adventurous demented man
I'm advisable so I advise you to watch how
closely you stand take these adverbs under
advisement for I need no advocate it's adventure
just to decipher all of the words that I spit

Judith Roche

HUNGER

All life born of hot thrust and eager
clinch is born to die
while those who come from
slow cell division can live forever.
The soul's flesh ripens
and chaffs, stretches and cramps,
caught in her confine.
Still, she must be amused
at her changing clothing, perhaps
enjoying it as theater, snake skin
high heels, gritty bars with big red wine,
a dusty lake gliding aside a lilac road.
The soul, always hungry, watches
the fleshy appetites and says
no, no that's not what I want,
but we, animal-ethereal alliances
that we are, break our hearts and health
trying to feed her what she cannot use
and does not want, her dark night
driving us to outrageous extremes,
while hunger, blind,
begging and nagging at us,
gnaws our flesh and leeches
our bones.

Roche

COUNTING THE CHROMOSOMES
—*for Robin*

What to say about it
that can be said

it is like every other
yet, like each, like no other

they're all different
we say to each other

though we know difference
as a matter of degree

not kind and when it's kind
we talk of rolls of the dice

luck and celestial pattern
reflected in biological code

which has to mean something
after all because everything does,

absurd as it all seems
at root, we laugh and consider

ourselves lucky to be so intimate
with a cosmic joke, singled out

for special consideration
and given so much to ponder

Roche

what love might learn
from the commonplace equation

the internal rhythm in the dance
when the dancer does not hear our music

and we know we are blessed
but, for fairness, not more than most

because all are amazing
in their own ways

though as time goes on
the even ones begin to seem

so like every other when he
is singular and unexpected

once I said all I ask
of life is that it surprise me

and I'll supply the passion
to meet it halfway

how I wake in the night
when he catches his breath

though I never remember it
and wonder how I know

mathematics is all and asymmetry
here is the depth of difference
in the palm of the hand

Roche

there are things we can count
in the outer garments of digits

and some know the inner gesture
from before they are born.

Roche

SILENCE

there he was, in the shadow
of the doorway again
some things he said and some

things he didn't say
in the daytime the dog
is gone again

and in the night, a shadow
appears in the doorway
and I lie perfectly still

that is the way of it
in the day he brings books
but the words tick in the clock

and stick in my eye
sound through my fingers
like bone hitting against stone

gone sad again
tie something to something else
and it becomes unraveled

from the center
like the shadows at night
this is the story of my life

on this bed
in this novel
in which I lie

David Romtvedt

TALKING WITH THE GOVERNOR AFTER THE JOHNSON COUNTY FAIR AND RODEO PARADE

I've been appointed poet laureate of my state.
Granted, it's the least populated state in the union
and one which many Americans can't place on a map.
Still, I could receive no greater honor.
But I offer few thanks and seem, I'm afraid,
not quite present. The fact is, I've been babysitting
a friend's dog while she's away in Denver
getting some culture. Someone has opened
the gate of my yard during the parade and the dog,
a long haired dachshund named Abby
whose ears fly like wings when she runs,
has disappeared. I imagine the screaming
and the sounds of gunshots—even though blanks—
the roar of motorcycles and diesel generators,
and the whining of the go-karts driven by middle aged men
in red fezs, have combined to terrify the dog.

She's gone and my friend is going to kill me,
poet laureate be damned. So I don't properly
thank the Governor, and disappear into the crowds
asking people if they've seen the lost dog.

A few hours later, a policeman comes by to tell me
he saw a little dog lying in the middle of the parade route
on her back as if sunbathing before the horses
arrived to crush her. He picked her up and put her in his house
and now he's brought her to me to see if she's the one.
"Yes." I shout in joy. But it's too late
to thank the Governor who is already gone.

Romtvedt

Well, poetry, they say that poetry is more often than not
against the ideals of normal social life.

And so the governor takes a risk—
not in naming me poet laureate, but in
naming anyone to such a post. The risk
isn't for what a person might do or say
but for poetry, what it is and might be.

Jillian Ross

A Small Poem De Contrapunta
—*In memory of Tamale who died in October 2003,*
three months after this poem was written.

TAMALE IS MY PUP
WITH A VANILLA CREAM CRESCENT-
BLACK STAR ON HER CHEST.
BROWN ACCENTS FLATTER HER
FURRY FACE.

El Manantial
La primordial nació en el mar.
La ola, la marea, el azul
Yo nací en una isla—
Escosia
Nací para bailar el ritmo del agua
y los cambios de la luna.

TAMALE IS FREE—SHE RUNS
ON THE FARM WHERE WE LIVE,
SNIFFS THE SCENT OF
APPLE BLOSSOMS, SWIMS
THE SKANKY IRRIGATION DITCH,
EATS POOP AND COMPOST
LIVING LIFE, JOY INCARNATE.

El Umbral
La jornada me empujó
de la cuna antes de
salir de la mamila.
Llegamos a la tierra
nueva de oro de California
Dejé a un pedazo de mi
alma afuera de mi—volar
encimame—como un globo
me siguió.

Ross

UNFENCED, UNFETTERED
BEAUTY, SHEPARD DOG GUARDS
MY BEDSIDE BY NIGHT
SMALL TO COYOTES AND CARS
SHE MAY DIE YOUNG BUT
NEVER BEFORE HER TIME.

El Crucero
Llegó el crucero
Y Dios mio! Veo que
tengo que escoger el camino
Primeramente—me quedó un rato
probar y provecho
el vino del olor de frambruesa
y tomar la sal de tu sudor. Conozco
las lagrimas de dolor pero
más los pasos del danzon.

TAMALE, INDEPENDENT
FIERCELY LOYAL FLIES
HIGH DIGS LOW
I LOVE HER COMPLETELY

La Montaña
Nací en una isla
La subida y bajada exista
por la marea y la
eternidad del agua—
No buscaba la montaña
de la piedra
Sin embargo
aqua esta ella y
aquí estoy yo

ME VOY!

Angel Ruiz

WORKING AT THE FIELDS

Working at the fields
trying hard to fill up the 3 ft. boxes
trying to get money for a car.

Making sure I put the ladder right
a couple of branches scrape my arms.
Working at the fields,

trying to fill up my bags with pears,
trying to hurry up and get paid,
trying to get money for a car,

trying to concentrate on what I'm doing.
Can't wait to leave,
working at the fields.

Getting back to work after lunch,
feeling tired, but thinking about my goal,
trying to get money for a car.

Still trying to fill up the 3 ft. boxes,
thinking about my goal,
working at the fields,
trying to get money for a car.

Ruiz

MÉXICO

La Huerta, Jalisco
Wishing to be there
That's where I'm from

Where you have tacos and tostados every day
My old home in
La Huerta, Jalisco

Watching drunk people in the streets
working and winning small change
That's where I'm from

Watching little kids working
that's how it is in my home
La Huerta, Jalisco

Makes me feel lucky here
but I'm still missing the place
where I'm from

Hoping to go back some day
so maybe I can help my family
La Huerta, Jalisco
that's where I'm from

Wendy Zárate S.

IF YOU HAD REMAINED

If you had remained
buried in my hair
sucking my soul out
of my neck

If your delayed breath
—drunk with desire—
had frozen my flesh
with fulfillment

If your eyes
If your latent pores
If your bittersweet fragrance

If, like an undeletable seal,
your footprints were still
on my sidewalk

If that day
you had left a diamond
written my inwards
that could with its reflection,
cover me with your warm shadow
Inside out
I would remember you,
I guess.

But I don't.

Manuh Santos

FORGOTTEN VOICE

My forgotten voice will arise once again,
this time, at this vivid moment. I am going

to stand firmly, to defend my forgotten
voice. I don't allow other voices to disturb and destroy
my right to spread out my voice.

My voice has shut since the God
has created me. Now I can't stand it
any more. My dream voice will not die as long
as my spirit lives to put this word to a notebook.

Santos

I Will Eat the Laws

I will eat the laws because I am a
free man. The laws are raining
like the rain from the vivid blue
clear sky. The laws are falling slowly.
Choose them. Politics and laws
are to keep people informed every single
day. Politicians, governments, follow
your orders you made and don't break
them. Use your judgment properly.
Listen to your heart and listen to the
society's voice. Don't ignore them, they
are part of your power. Everyone has
a voice to hear. Don't judge me
now because you don't know my real world.

I am going to eat the politician's
laws because it was given by them.
I can eat them because I was born
naturally inside my mother's stomach.
I was created freely inside my mom's
body. My mom is the only person
that can apply rules on me. So you
don't have any right toward me. So
I am going to create my own laws which
are going to apply better on me than
the politician's laws which are
not natural.

I can write my own laws on the
blue sky where the politicians can't

Santos

reach it. I am a free man. I
clearly think. If I want to follow
my order I just fly over the society
and read my constitutions to myself.

People wake up. Why are you sleeping
too much? The birds are singing outside.
The early dews are falling down on the
ground giving life to the dying grass.
The son is coming up to give you light,
to give you hopes and dreams. Get up.
Open your eyes widely. Listen attentively.
Go out and see the sun's light, feel
it. Escape the darkness. Don't be
afraid to see the sun. Sun does not
judge. Sun is for everyone. It is time
for you to see the sun. It is time for you
to change your ideas because
you are free and let's change the
world. I'd rather destroy the
border than go to Iraq.

Santos

300 B. C.
EXPERIENCE DESTROYS INNOCENCE

Some people live happy and others come to
destroy their right to live anywhere they
want. Their voices don't reach another side
of the mountain. These are forgotten voices.
People are born with natural right and others
came to destroy without looking closely
to your eyes. Then you are naive and others
are cunning. They hate you because you don't
[   ] to show. When people see you the way
you are, people judge you without knowing
you. Then people take over your dream.

Santos

The Land of Immigration
—to Jim Bodeen

I must believe this is a land of
migration. Where many human beings
are looking for. What are you thinking?
Ask yourself, Where did your ethnicity come
from? I can say, all you came from the
continent of Europe, or other parts of
the world. This is the land that welcomes
people. What would have happened if the
Statue of Liberty was built in California?
I am more than this land because my
ancestors were here before all other races—
What right do I have now? None, because
you committed a crime by taking away all
my liberty, my hope, and my freedom
to walk any direction I want to. I wanna
know where is my right? Who broke it and
why are you so tender to see my eyes? Now
I am still a slave. Maybe no, maybe yes.
I believe I exist in this world and I am part
of what you see and do. I live to tell the stories.

Santos

THE WALL

Border's wall separates my love to Mom.
That wall defeats my dream. You know
in some ways I feel I am put to jail. That
wall is making me to forget my Mom because
I have not seen her side, seven year exclusive.
I feel the love for my mom is dying
little by little. You know I love my Mom
very much, but the thing is, I can't see my
Mom because of that wall. I wish that wall did not
exist, so we all can go anywhere we want
to go. I can't defend my little dream.

Jane Sarmiento Schwab

HOP FIELDS, 1944
—*for Frank*

You told me of first summers in Yakima:
family knotting strands of string
hanging from hop vines
to make the fattest balls that
thinned into braids in winter by small hands.

Side glances told you which family member
grabbed the daily prize—a long twine
wound around and around
by arms already tired from cutting.

You worked in fields not your own
dreamed of a six foot reach,
unending twine
circling a globe you'd craft
to shade your family from the August sun.

Jo Shafer

RED STOVE

Stranded in a strange airport
in a foreign city
with no money
no passport
no ID
I refused to panic.
It happened so fast I never noticed
until it was too late.
Whom to call?
Nobody.
Didn't know anybody.
Not here, anyway.

I approached the counter
and asked for traveler's aid
or something like that.
Sorry, ma'am.
You'll have to wait.
Storm outside
flights stacked
and we're booked.
Out of the throng two women drifted up to me
and bobbed politely
almost timidly.
We'll help you.
They took me home
warm and dry
and fed me soup from a red stove.
Tell us a story, they said.

I told them about two little sisters

Shafer

Chinese girls with long black hair
tangled from another rain
and their mother
abandoned in a strange land
with no money
no passport
no clothes except what they wore.
I took them home with me
warm and dry
and fed them strange food from my white stove.

While the mother spread my extra blankets
to make pallets for the night
I hung the little girls' dresses on chair backs
and dried their hair by the fire.
I told them stories until they fell asleep.
The mother watched me closely
almond eyes washed in worry.
Neither spoke the other's words
only subliminal messages
all night long
while outside
incessant drizzle
streaked black windows like silent tears.

Next day
a sparkling morning held damp promises
of fresh starts
and new beginnings.
I sent the little girls and their doe-eyed mother
on their way with all I could spare
but she would take no more
than she could tie together in a blue and white
tablecloth.

Shafer

The little girls danced and skipped
around puddles reflecting cerulean blue.
Just before they turned the corner,
they stopped to smile back at me.
I waved good-bye
and they were gone.
I never saw any of them again.

Always wondered
about those little girls.

Zev Shanken

ISRAEL 2004 WITH 30 TEENAGERS
A CLASS TRIP TO YAD V'SHEM, ISRAEL'S
HOLOCAUST MEMORIAL MUSEUM

The secret is out.
It can be done.
You can get away with it.
You can be cruel beyond victory.
Nothing stands in your way
if you're smart and strong
and avoid strategic blunders.
The secret of the holocaust
is that it can be done.

I told this to a gentle student
who replied, "They didn't get away with it.
Look around."
I kept my rejoinder to myself.

DIZENGOFF SQUARE

Countries
don't know
how small they are.

There are no
maps
in sidewalk cafes.

Shanken

THOSE '65–'68 JOURNALS

that I never turned into that book
have become my psychic Ur-text
for teaching.
I'm trying to get my students
to do the '65 work for me.
All the adolescent layers
and god and religion
and sex and later poor Zak Berkowitz
and civil rights, ironies in everyday life,
pop music and sensitive conflicts of identity—
it's all in my arc of lesson plans on Israel.

2 A.M. BLIZZARD

Shouts on the streets from
Maimonides to King George.
Rugs of falling ice.
Wind sings off key.

TOLD TO SMALL GROUP OF STUDENTS ON SHABBAT

God is a metaphor
for the power of goodness.
It feels like
  it can move mountains.
It feels like
  it began the world.
It feels like it gives
     strength to the weary
     sight to the blind
     pride to the lowly
     lessons to the proud
     glory to Israel
     splendor to all that exists.
But it's only a metaphor?
Yes, but what ideas aren't?

The students were silent.
Then Jeff said,
"That's really good."
Later I learned he'd lost his mother on 9/11.

Shanken

THE WISDOM OF SOLOMON

Not which woman is the true mother,

but which one would make the better one.

Even if Solomon were wrong,

the child would be in good care.

Not whether Abraham would kill his son,

but whether he knew this new God well enough

to know that he was supposed to protest.

He failed the test. God bailed him out.

Not that the fire did not consume the bush,

but that bushes usually burn. No, not even that:

That there is such a thing as a bush, as fire.

Things exist. Facts are miracles.

Derek Sheffield

BREATHING IN WARTIME

A glass bowl magnifies two pupils
bulging mutely
as a goldfish peers beyond its water,

perhaps to the windows of the next building
where a man in dress shirt and tie
appears, gathers papers from a desk, disappears.

The goldfish makes O's with thin lips,
stubborn little O's, wordless howls
I mimic by opening and closing my mouth.
Reflected in the windows

where the desk remains empty, a jet
ripples, shrinks and stretches,
its tail fin catching the light, flaring
spikes of a silent explosion.

Sheffield

BODY COUNT

The bright weapons that sing in the atmosphere, ready to
pulverize the cities of the world, are the dreams of giants
without a center. Their mathematical evolutions are hieratic
rites by Shamans without belief.
—Thomas Merton

They could not reach us
at first. They were nothing, silhouettes
we fired at. I got one, I said
to the ones on my side who could not stop
their rifles from drawing line after parallel line,
whose eyes were decimal points.

Then faces filled the shadows.

In room after room, we lie.
From the half-light of one,
I listen for bedsprings and floorboards.
How many? I cannot stop
aiming for accuracy, adding the two
minus a leg, four less something more.

Formulaic: each pair of lungs

expands so many times per hour.
If I could only breathe
without sound, snuff that bloody racket
circling beneath my skin,
that quivering muscle
making zero after zero after zero.

THE FIREFIGHTERS WALK INTO MOUNTAIN SPORTS

Straight from flames, faces soot-slapped
and yellow jackets swishing,
they track ashes of century-wide pines
wrenched from root-sockets
and sucked skyward like bungled fireworks.
A blaze in their ears, they shout across aisles
and racks, thumbs hooked over belts
with curious assurance: whether they hold
picks and shovels, or Polartec and Nike, the end
will come nameless, wearing the same face.

One models a hat, and they hoot.
If they wanted, they could howl
at such prices, or the well-tanned skier
in search of a deal and a fit
clomping seven times across the store
in a pair of orange Atomics.

Slim and pig-tailed, the girl
who rips their receipts from the register
is the last sight and line they walk
before flinging again comets of earth
at something like the sun unhinged.
From their radio a staticky voice calls,
the green world widening into darkness.

A luggage full

ins, stained

he would have

it.

has no desire,

er there

rs, clutching

d her shoulders.

e will come

spell

animal,

d.

Harald Sigmar

YOU AND I ARE ALONE IN THE WORLD

You and I are alone in the world
        Surrounded by friends everywhere
                It's a warm and wonderful feeling

Our children have gone on their own
        Each to a separate life
                You and I are alone in the world

We've been together for sixty years
        In one way or another
                It's a warm and wonderful feeling

Karen Sigmar Mason

FIFTIETH WEDDING ANNIVERSARY

Fifty years, fifty years…
Imagine fifty years together.
Thirty-nine is the most
I can truly understand.
Fifty years to tiny children
must seem forever, without end.

If I were a quilter, I'd sew a fine quilt
with a quilt piece for every year.
It wouldn't be neat little rows of squares,
but a crazy quilt from snatches of fabric
collected wherever you've lived,
brown velvet from Saskatchewan earth.

White lace from Dakota snow.
Brick raw silk from Pennsylvania.
Bluest satin you've ever seen from Seattle
skies, with a splash of Puget Sound green.
Wheaten linen from Manitoba fields.
From Kelso, a gray, misty flannel—and

from Iceland, finest wools of mossy green,
with eider down between.
Vancouver the thread, Tacoma the needles,
Yakima, the vision to place it together.
And now, in Seattle, it would lay on your bed
with the warmth of completeness.

But I know you find warmth
in the fabric of images
and the thread of words as well.

Sigmar Mason

For we are a clan of many air quilters,
and for each of your fifty years
I have a piece of story, bright as laughter, soft as tears.

June 15, 1990

Bill Siverly

CONFLUENCE

October tenth, eighteen–five, Clark found the Kimooenem
Greenish-blue, the KoosKooskee "clear as cristial."
"Imediately in the point is an Indian Cabin...
Not one Stick of timber near the forks and but fiew trees above.
Indians came down to the river on horses to view us
descending."

Lewis and Clark did not yet imagine the Snake
Could be the main stream, so they named it Lewis's River.
They camped upon the north bank a mile below the forks
To take astronomical reckonings, but night proved cloudy:
Latitude forty-six degrees, twenty-five minutes.

One hundred thirty-eight years, one month and three days later
At eleven-fifteen a.m. on that same confluent latitude,
The one who is making this poem was born:
Born without mythology, born without history,
The present moment extended to every horizon.

Returning upriver May fourth, eighteen–six,
Lewis and Clark camped four miles below the Clearwater,
Next day trudged preoccupied past the confluence,
And paid no further attention to the place
Where towns would rise bearing their names.

Camping by Yakto´inu, the band near Arrow Junction,
Where a single lodge held thirty families,
Lewis tried to convince old men he had not come to kill them.
The Captains presented Cut Nose a Jefferson medal,
And KoosKooskee ran all night long like clear Coyote laughter.

Judith Skillman

THE FAMILY GOAT

We like to love him despite the smell
of his goatishness. On good days
he stands on top of the makeshift house
and roars. On bad days he has eaten

whatever it was we were saving for ourselves.
This could be indicative of a certain
obstreperousness—his tendency
to act like a child with the horns

that need rubbing, yet can be rubbed
the wrong way. When we bleed
as a result of flaying him with our words
the blood runs dark and wet, not

orange and dry like Christ's.
We like to say *he should know better*
even when our condition has never been worse.
He is happy to goad us, to become

ever more goat-like, to sleep in the green swath
between the shed and the masterpiece
that was once our home. There a moon came
and went, a scentless object no one could touch

until the night he refused the solace of escape,
and tore certain objets d'art from the walls.
Unlike the elephant who occupied
our closet, with its spit of a tail, this goat

Skillman

was unable to accept our feverish
attempts at affection. Cowed
but never cowering, he hid in corners
frayed by wear. His misdeeds multiplied.

As if it were not enough merely to stink,
to be stuck with relentless germs, wills, and years,
we squandered our best stores on him.
He remained obstinate, unruly

in his refusal to take on the role of middle child,
father, husband. More like death
than any person, he continues to eat his way
through the holes in our memories.

Skillman

HEAT LIGHTNING

That to which we were beholden
as children. I remember the silent flicker
in clouds of gauze, how we,
banished to a closet-sized room,
lay flat-chested on iron bunks.

Voices outside. The scuttled car
returning a grown woman
to her home. The whole world desperate
and she, in heels,
clicked up the sidewalk and turned a key.

Maybe it was the mystery
of her womanhood, her fullness,
to be revealed with the next silent firework.
Or perhaps what the heat meant
was sweat, and sleeplessness.

It showed things as they were—
dishes crusted over,
pots black enough to take a flash of blue
when we snuck down
in the kitchen.

Each stroke of light dull as the moon
hidden behind the sheet
the woman would be lying under,
in her grown-up house joined to ours.
There the man would turn slightly

Skillman

in his sleep, sensing her perfume, her lingerie,
imagining she had been out with the girls,
not bothering to wake or talk.
She, our mascot, magnet, compass rose,
might lie under the spell of idolatry for years.

So what if she never needed to tell the truth,
which was, after all, nothing more
than a blur, a white lie
leftover from a series of days
above ninety degrees.

Skillman

Magpie Eyes

Whatever shines
or is lost like the moon,
that yellow—

a glint of nostalgia, the train
in passing, the bells and ropes,
what I want is not that.

All I've seen
is black as obsidian,
friable as sodalite.

From Brazil came cross-sections of geode,
from my parents came arithmetic,
algebra, parameters.

From a studio of kitsch
I gunnysacked diagonal tulips
and bridge spans.

Whatever shone I befriended—
coins, diamonds, strands of pearls
cultured in fresh water, salt water.

The world was plural.
I bought a bouclé coat in winter white.
What I saw was what I needed.

There wasn't time for sleep.
Debt rose like water.
My husband, the collector,

Skillman

slipped away from me
clutching a pillar, his eyes
blue-green.

I think it was in peace time he left,
and then it was yesterday
or tomorrow, the year of war

and wooden nickels.
One by one my charms grew legs:
quartz elephant, horse, owl, turtle

moving slowly as the earth.
That's when I took my butterfly net
and walked on up the ridge.

I can't tell you what I caught there.
It was rare
and not popular enough to keep.

Ann Spiers

On the Gulf of Tonkin Between Wars, 2004

Hired dockside, the wood boat holds us.
Red sunset loses its rancor, and we float
in that moment when no port awaits us,
no land owns us, no aircraft strafes us,
and our names are on no list to live or die.

We have nothing to do, rocking into dark,
but be flesh and bone riding the top deck.
Gentled, we jettison enmity into waters
once boiling with five-inch shells and salted
with blood carried by the Red River into the sea.

The sky's blue fails. The moon grins.
The *Turner Joy* returns, phantom ship,
masts clotted with communication gear.
In a flash of time, she is gone.
We forget history, and history releases us

as wind moves water across this wet battlefield,
as silenced air fills with stars,
and the seam holding day and night disappears.

Clemens Starck

NEIGHBORS

New neighbors
building a house up on the hill…
She raises goats. He works at the pen.
From my back door
it's thirty miles, as the crow flies,
over the mountains to the coast. It used to be
I could imagine
walking it—unimpeded.
No fences. Nothing but deer trails and logging roads.

Now I'm surrounded by neighbors.

Which is better: seeking the recluse
in the mountains, and finding he's not at home,
or helping the goat-lady
rig up a new wooden pedestal
for our mailboxes?

Erik M. Stevens

Some Conversations Are Not Random Occurrences
—for Christina

I wake with tears
my wrists tender
You were not in my dreams
but I thought of you
You teenaged, 15, 16, 17,
I don't know exactly how old
I know your first name
but not your last
I don't remember the exact color of your hair
somewhere between blonde or brown
slightly long?
I'm not good with physical descriptions
I remember your smile
I remember thinking you would have more
to talk about than the latest trip
to the shopping mall
Something more than boys, clothes, and music.

You were overweight
and I knew you were not
the most popular girl at school
These things are written in the shadow
across a face
the slope of a shoulder
But you were the one
among that group of teenagers
that I thought
I'd like to know her better.

Stevens

Months later, the mother of the two sisters
you were visiting
talks to me
about the daughters
the friends they left behind
You
You were in that conversation
and I learned that you slashed your wrists once.

So I awake with tears
sadness, anger
that such pain can exist
You know that weight matters
looks matter
the style of hair
fit of clothes
clear skin
it all matters
My words
my tears
do they matter?

When I turned thirty
I realized I had never expected
to live so long
What age will you be
when you realize
you hadn't expected to live so long?
Such freedom
Such a blessing
New life
unexpected, unhoped for
Can you make it to that point?
To not know the future
is such agony.

PRINTER'S INK

I

Seven AM, Monday morning
we punch in, struggle to remember
what jobs need finishing from Friday.
Pete has been working the paper cutter
for two hours, an economic series of movements
cutting reams of paper to fit the small letterpress.
Janice runs a lift of pamphlets through the folder,
stops, adjusts the second fold, and then settles in
for a long session of feeding the clattering machine.
With Tracy and Gina on the other side of the room
I begin a hand job, assembling a packet of instructional cards,
sealing flaps of folders, the cards tucked inside.

Soon it will be time
to make a cup of tea
with water that is never hot enough
and always tastes of coffee, no matter
how many times we wash the pot.

II

We tuck, fold, score, laminate,
watch pallets of blank sheets of paper
get fed into the rectangular mouth of the paper cutter.
Pete's thumbs on the controls, his foot pressing
the pedal to lower the clamp
before the wide blade arcs down
trimming 2000 sheets of paper in ten seconds.
Roll the trimmed paper down to the pressroom,

roll the printed sheets back up to the bindery.
Start the process all over again.
Paper in all hues and textures,
glossy, matte, water marked, card stock, linen, 3–part forms,
envelopes, die cut stickers and labels.

In the midst of this world of paper and ink
in that cluttered, windowless space
we talk, discuss,
spin out stories, dream aloud.
We.
Not the whole crew
but the we of memory,
Janice, Gina, Tracy and I.

III

While still eighteen
I move out,
take a couple duffle bags of clothes,
several boxes of books.
The timid housemate of Janice,
one month only,
a grey and rainy November.
By the time I become Janice's temporary housemate
I know she is gay,
knowledge come to me slowly, dimly,
not proclaimed loudly.
She assumed I was a lesbian as well,
the levels of knowing and unknowing stretching
into time, past and future,
my avowal I like boys,
her perception that it is only a matter of time
and I will come out of the closet.

Stevens

She is older, older than Tracy and Gina,
who also assume in the beginning that I am a dyke.
What do they see in me that I do not?

IV

I will start college after one year working
with paper, working with women who love women.
I will read Søren Kierkegaard,
learn to speak Swedish,
take women's studies and anthropology classes.
Janice, who is a press operator as well as a bindery worker,
will find work with another printing company.
We will rarely see one another.
I will stay in touch with Tracy and Gina for a time,
then there will be one too many moves,
too much time passed
and I will no longer think of them.

V

Why does tea that tastes of coffee
bother me so much?
The blurring of one thing
with that which it is not.
What I am on the outside
is not what I am on the inside.
The name I answered to as a child
is not the name I answer to now.
Am I like one of those sheets of paper,
trimmed once,
fed multiple times through the big 4-color press
until the separate layers of ink
become that magical full color?

Stevens

Trimmed again to the finished size
folded perhaps
or laminated
or perfect without any further work
by the bindery crew,
ready to be boxed and delivered.

This is what all of us want
the adult self to be the completion
of the child self
full color,
exactly as the mockup and layout
intended it to be.

No one wants to be the sheet
that jams the press,
the one tossed in the recycle bin,
the register off,
the blue too dark,
too many hickeys from unseen specks
of dirt on the printing press drum.

VI

It is Friday night at Janice's house,
Tracy a lighter and more relaxed presence
than her partner Gina.
Janice taking the occasional break
to sit on the windowsill
smoke her Marlboro.
A few other friends there, names now forgotten,
a circle of women
eating pizza
talking
laughing.

Stevens

Who is it that first says to me,
of course, you're a lesbian?
Does it matter now?
The whole circle agrees,
laughs when I tell them no.

VII

Fifteen years later
I go from one thing to the other.
First female,
now male.
Smugly I assume that the closet
I needed to come out of
was for my gender, not my sexuality.
I like men, I say.

And yet.
There is no man in my life.
There are only women.
Friends
flirting
using that somewhat swishy tone of voice
I've heard gay men use
believing my heart is safe.

Now it's more than twenty years later.
Of course, you're a lesbian.
What do they see in me that I don't?

Ed Stover

Homecoming: 1950

I see it clearly,
the way it was,
the way I want it to be,
with the daylight dying against the hills,
and the valley below filling with dark.
We arrive from the southeast,
the lights of the Kaiser combing
the fringes of fields tired from harvest.
Mother speaks, her voice soft in the air
like the wings of nighthawks.

"They will be expecting us," she says.

Father is quiet. In the backseat,
my sisters and I dream a moment
of things remembered forever:
The billboard that reads
"Yakima Valley: Fruit Bowl of the Nation,"
the smokestack of the sugarbeet factory,
the living screen of the Starlite Drive-In
where the main feature has begun,
everything larger than life, all of us
images moving across a landscape.

Like finding landfall after years at sea—
the line on the horizon
at first hazy and indistinct,
then the details, the shimmering
browns and greens,
everything in living color
against a backdrop of sky,

Stover

the moment of arriving somewhere
after leaving somewhere else
where something has been decided.

Even now, revisiting this moment,
I am waiting for what it means—
the valley at dusk,
this town with its streets and people,
my leaning forward in the seat,
peering over Father's shoulder,
hearing Mother's words in the air like wings:
"They will be expecting us," she says.

The Face in the Window

The face in the window
belongs to a woman
bent to a task,
her hands busy
below the glass
with the dishes,
the ironing,
her sewing perhaps,
or is it her life,
the scattered remnants of which
she sorts and re-sorts,
trying to find sense
in the nonsense of it all?
Yes, she seems to say,
pausing in thought,
then, frowning,
she redoubles herself,
leans into it,
the grease, or the regret,
the something said a long time ago
that came to her in the night
so that she rose ever so quietly
to come here and remind me,
an early-morning passerby,
of my own scattered life,
the faces that follow me,
the promises made and broken,
that know my secrets,
how I seek solace
on these solitary walks,

Stover

but no matter how I atone
it is never enough,
no, it's too late for that,
and now my recriminations
find a home in this face
in this window
which suddenly looks up
and out as if to ask:
What else could I have done?

Joseph Stroud

My Lord What a Morning
When the Stars Begin to Fall

I wake before dawn, and sense my house
around me, its skeleton of fir I framed
years ago, back in the time when I believed
I could make a shelter, back in my pride,
when I boxed out a skylight so I might
watch the stars cross over me each night.

laying it do

in this house
in this life
next to yours.

Jenni N
3-16

Loren Sundlee

BACKING

Nights in fall,
crops cut to stubble,
with moon for eyes,
Terry and I flushed pheasants
along field roads.
Where no fences cribbed us
we couldn't tell row from road
and zigzagged, crossplowed all symmetry,
our butts hardly seating
the bench of the bouncing Dodge.

Years later while paving a road,
with the perfect blindness of hindsight,
he backed a truck over a man,
and when he found him,
tongue and eyes reaching for space
his chest begrudged, Terry's cry
cut through the hot rock of builders' brains,
clung like tar and flattened
a lane one way.

Now when his son takes the wheel
Terry's palms refuse to dry.
He drives dark, pathless fields,
surges wild amid scattering wings,
sure of nowhere when
everywhere is road.

Abril Talavera

LONELY NIGHTS

Sitting down below a tree,
dark night,
only billions of candles on.
Trying to blow very hard
to turn them out
so I could not see
your empty space.
I hope you help me
with those candles,
because you are
nearer to them.

Molly Tenenbaum

MUSIC, FLOWERS, WORDS LIKE RAIN

Reverse to before I loved these
when the smallest note
spread like sugar in tea
before I grew
a petal or played
before I said
a thing

that counted
breathe once breathe
twice garden glove
polished to my palm
gone the banjo
with flowerpot
inlay gone three times
the Blackwing
pencils gone

round mouth
taking breath
back in
four times takes
itself back in

a brush comes clearing across the air
washes it the color it already is

Barbara L. Thomas

YELLOW BELL

Not blessed with feathers
Of our own,
We array ourselves
And our nests
With decorative flourishes—
Weeds
From the pasture
Arranged
On a table.
A grandchild's gift
Of a single
Roadside blossom,
A bower of fragrance—
The canary-yellow bell
Captured in a bit of blue-flowered china.

Thomas, B

WIND SPIRIT

O Spirit of Wind
Spirit of Wind
Wind Spirit
Wind
Wind
Spirit

Bring me word
Of the sky
Sky People
Dark side
Secrets
Moon
People

O Spirit of Wind
Spirit of Wind
Wind Spirit
Wind
Wind
Spirit

Bring me word
Of the water
Water People
Sound the green
Spawn
Water
People

Thomas, B

Sing me a song
Of the earth
Land People
Sing willow leaf
And bud
Land
People

Spirit of Wind
Sky People
Spirit of Wind
Water People
Wind
Wind
Spirit

Spirit of wind
Sky secrets
Water spawn
Budding willow
O Earth
Earth
People

O Spirit of Wind
Spirit of Wind
Wind Spirit
Wind
Wind
Spirit

Stephen Thomas

●

PERSPECTIVAL

Everything was different
when I remember.
Taller, farther, stranger,
more to be desired,
everything hurt worse
and lasted longer:
high up in the tree
time was more like oil,
less like gasoline.

Except for falling. That's
the opposite. What
used to be a blurred green rush
goes now
more slowly, is
viscous, more
eventful.

Alexa Torres

The Star That Guides Me
—*for my grandfather, Raul Torres*

The story has been told on many occasions
A baby girl held in her grandpa's arms.
She gazes towards the warmth and brightness of the star.
A reflection of herself in his eyes she sees.
The promise is made "I will always protect you."
He would give his life for her: the promise would be tested.
Even though his eyes see no more
The star shines brighter than ever before.

Torito—Raul Torres

MIDNIGHT

One day the doctor told me that I was blind.
The next thing I knew is that people were treating me different.
I really don't know why.
but I think that I have a pretty good idea as to why.
And following is my answer to those people.

I am a blind person.
Yes, a blind person.
Note, I still have feelings
Like everyone else.
My feelings are hurt
When I see people
Shy away from me
as if I have a contagious disease.
I can understand people
Who don't know me doing that.
But, people that I know are
Doing the same thing.
My own relatives are or
Seem to be afraid of me.
Some people look at me
And say, Poor man
He lost his sight
As a result of
A heart transplant.
They don't realize that
I am still the same person as before.
Yes, don't pity me.
Accept me for what
I am. A blind person
With the same needs as

Torito

Everyone else.
Look at me.
Yes, I am blind.
Look at me. What do you see?
I hope that you see
A person just like you. Yes look at me.
And think about what
You would like a person
You don't know to be like.
Then, think of what you would like others to
See as you and think of when they look at you.
Yes , I am a blind person
And I probably will be
Until the day that
I no longer exist. But, until then
I will endure—
Endure the looks that
I will get.
The looks of fright
From those that
Don't realize that
There are people
Who are different
and who live life
The best they can.
Yes, I am blind.
And I refuse to be a burden to anyone.
I do not want to be
on any kind of relief.
I still have most of my senses
And can still work.
So give me a chance.
I know that
You will not be sorry.

Torito

CIEGO

For my relatives and friends—
Yes, I am not the same
No one is always the same
From one minute to another
I know that it's hard
For you not to pity me
Because I also pity you
Because you don't understand
That in actuality I am the same person
Who was supposedly normal
Like you
Yes, I am different
Than all of you
But I still have feelings
The same feelings
That I had before I changed
I breathe, eat, and drink
Have emotions, hurt and cry
Yes, I still know how to love
I still love all of you
I cannot understand
Why you pity me so
Also, don't be afraid of me
My blindness
Will not pass on to you
Like most contagious diseases
If you don't want to visit me
Call me, I can still talk
And you won't have to keep on guard
Because you are afraid
That you will make a

Torito

Mistake and show your emotions
I am not afraid
To talk about myself
Ask me questions
That you have about how I feel
About the results
Of my surgery
I'll still consider you
And everyone else my friends
If I knew you before
I know what you look like
To me, you will always look
Like you did before
And, if I didn't know you before
I have the ability
To formulate what you look like
By your actions and attitude
I have a great self-esteem and attitude
Even after all that has happened
But I still need hugs and kisses
And other kinds of warm fuzzies
Yes, I am blind
And I am alive and wanting
To help anyone
Who needs me to help them.

Ann Tweedy

THE FULL PULSE OF HAPPINESS

when i was in elementary school,
i watched girls and guys gather
in big old impalas and cutlasses
in the dirt lot behind george's cleaners.
back then the prettiest girls in the world
worked as cashiers at the supermarket—
but the rest of them were here

walking home from the grocery,
the five and dime, the train station,
after dark my mother and i would see them:
sitting in cars parked close
together, smoking, eating donuts,
drinking beer. the girls wore
tight designer jeans and spaghetti
strap tank tops. now and then, they'd ride
down north main with their boyfriends,
streaking on lipstick and shadow, brushing
swaths of permed hair. my mother thought
it was impolite for a girl to groom
in front of her boyfriend, but i doubted
politeness could get you anywhere

sometimes the mother of a kid that lived
near my babysitter was there, and sometimes
the kid too. she was a year or so younger
than me. the mother sat in a car
while the kid stood outside drinking soda
or eating packaged ice cream. an open car window
siphoned the mother's crimped voice:

Tweedy

tara, get over here. still, i couldn't help
but envy the girl—she got to watch
and, if that wasn't enough, they bought her
all the bite-sized pleasures a kid could bear

WHAT ARE MY LINES?

Pluma en mano. ¿Quien soy yo?
¿Qué es lo qué sé?

I am a woman.Vivo la vida de todas las mujeres.
I am peaceful but have opinions.
I can submit and break free.

Me:
It all is beauty.
No need to request explanations.
Just the sun warming my Mexican blood.
Being me is enough.
Give love and respect.
Wearing my 6 dollar flip-flops is plenty.
La vida vuelve a ser un viaje.
I will not talk about politics.

Other me:
I don't know a thing.
All I thought I knew is weird.
I then hold the record for the most entangled world of thoughts.
The forces inside me make me walk away.
Necesito un lugar donde ser.
I will not talk about politics.

Could I scream out "Bi-polar?"
Can't I just be more simple?
Think simple?
Vivo la vida de todas las mujeres.
I always know that God is real.

Mary Ann Waters

ALTHOUGH IT WAS LATE IN THE SEASON

I stopped at the market to buy bedding plants,
impatiens, geranium, pansy, the word bed
so capable of shifting its allegiance

from adjective to noun to verb.
Do you see how I stumble?
When I thought to pay the proprietor

he was eyeing me with concern.
Tulips, he said, something now for spring.
I told him I was not prepared

for the expectations of bulbs.
Will your absence always fill me this way?
I drove to the racetrack, hoping there

to find loss so exact I could count it,
when luck, that clown,
smiled with his mouth full of money.

In the clamor, I was a winner,
a student of this small truth: there is
no compensation. The sky was grey as tin.

I expected nothing more.
But as I was driving home, an ease
descended, not unlike fatigue.

At least I felt myself succumbing,
though I held to the steering wheel
as we say sometimes
for dear life.

Waters

ON THE TRAIL

No wonder at the top there was nothing
to say. Daisies we could understand,
either we loved each other
or we didn't.
Even sunflowers, those bright yea-sayers,
and the single 'oh'
of the nearly-transparent lily.
Why, we could discuss forget-me-nots
and walk away.

But this snow plant, this lone stalk
of red flames pushing up
red through the pine needles, red
through the filtered light, held us
with its single command.

To descend into a flower is first to think:
petal, pistil, stamen
and then to forget.
To descend into a flower is to wallow
in pollen, is to hum with the need
to take without apology,
to use and to abandon.

We had been ready to turn, and go back.
But then there was no going back, and
no going back ever, and then
not wanting to go back.

Amber Wherry

DREAMTIME

slip into picture static
stare at patterns long enough
they resolve from chaos imagining
light show of the subconscious
in relief on the eyelids
sink further
into room of your soul
lost objects, memories, people
some doors stand open
some need a push
others a key
filled with liberty to wonder
not for ordinary consumption

mad artist of your brain
subconscious paints dreamtime tableau
jump into unknown universe
that sometimes put in real life experiences
some scenes never appear in culture
fragile, ephemeral, frightening
some cross over my way
a name here, a shape or color there
a half remembered tune

Wherry

triggered
flashback rush of chemical sequence
washes over reality
some dreams are movies
break through daylight
with vivid detail, bizarre imagery
nonsensical brainstew
that makes sense only to the owner

telling dreams is pale imitation
to total sensory immersion
Technicolor super Dolby sound
more terrifying, more gratifying than life
yet you always wake up

Mary Whitechester

DEATH

land-mines a naive vessel
deep in your wife's brain—
wrestles her true heartbeat
to a standstill, breath
ceased   Lurches
your pallid uncle to his knees
Stalks the rooms of
your sister's burning house
Death polishes the sharp teeth
of suicide—gone: father
lover author husband
safety of living

Attentive companion
incautious as love
Pull the word into your mouth—
taste death
roll it against your teeth

Let death slice your tongue
Get used to it

John Willson

GESTURE IN GOTHIC
—Mary's Chapel, Frankenberg an der Eder, Germany

Angels, their stone faces battered
off in Lutheran zeal, twelve in a row,
play harps and violins along a ledge.
I draw my thumb across a stone harp string.
Outside, a truck diesels into the morning,

and light from high windows carves
shadows in the robes of saints who stand here,
beheaded, two on either side of the niche
where Mary once stood, *Virgo Maria*
chiseled below it. Alone,

without faith, in this one-pew, soaring
room, am I the only figure intact?
No. In a corner beside the dark
window that adjoins the cathedral,
three ceiling arches fall to a demon's

back, the demon astride a burgher, clutching
his ears and hair. Both face outward,
the demon's beard brushing the burgher's head,
the burgher slightly crouched, hands on thighs,
his mouth grimly set as though he must,

yet cannot, close his eyes.
What has kept them undefaced?
What keeps me in the sad chapel

Willson

except for my own sadness? A light,
not of morning, gathers against the stone
firmament of the empty niche,
substance within shadow,
suffused presence made
palpable by the figure's absence.
Out of my pocket I pull a crescent-shaped

sliver of abalone shell, talisman
from boyhood. In my open palm,
for no reason I can imagine,
I hold it one moment under that light
then turn toward the door's iron latch.

Willson

THE SON WE HAD

Pregnancy's first estrogen arouses you
the way Sunday morning bacon's aroma pulls me
from slumber, and wild with dormant hunger
you gorge on the hormonal surge inside
her left breast. Six weeks later
we miscarry, and with our fingers

find we carry you, a lump hard
at gestation north of the nipple.
On delivery the surgeon pronounces you
highly mitotic, healthy for your kind,
and we have you, our one and only,
a malignant baby bastard. I jumble
sounds from the word *disease*

and name you Sidney.
Something left of you inside
feels the kitchen growing hot
with radiation and rumors of richer tissue.
Oh Sidney, ungrateful son, you strike

out, leaving us no word.
You turn up in the liver,
a one-centimeter X ray ghost, and I give you
your own last name: Havoc.
Where have we failed, Sidney Havoc, that you
punish us with arrogance? What would it take

Willson

for you to know our grief, our love?
We send you the best in care
packages express, marked *chemo:*
Cytoxan
Adriamycin
5-Fluorouracil—5FU for short—*Fuck You*
Five Times, Sidney, it hurts that much.
If you could watch your mother's hair

falling over you, would you lose
your immunity to our sorrow?
Already your pimply sneer grows
smaller, receding in the crowd of normal
cells, until we no longer see you.
Yet however bereft and guilty of bad
parenthood these seven months, we know
better than to mourn
you, cocksure boy.

Vince Wixon

FLOOD TOWN

That town along the river, the one
with the slaughterhouse on the flood plain
where every thirty years carcasses
and rubber boots float along the loading dock
and eddy in flotsam and sewage
while sides of beef inside hang on hooks
tracking above the muck. Workers
slide open the metal doors so the water
can head to where it had in mind
from the beginning.

Every time the levee is rebuilt.
The city fathers say as the water rises,
"She'll hold this time. Those boulders, concrete,
that rebar. We did it right this time."
But water can wait—the snow
piling up in the mountains,
then rain—high and low,
long and warm.

At the Friendly Tavern, workers
take a break from sandbagging,
rescuing dogs in motorboats, hustling
sump pumps for the bowling alley, and sit
on the stools, their feet up, and drink bottled beer.
Peanut shells seek the main channel,
empty pop cases nose the bar railing.
The drinkers compare earthquakes, landslides,
tornados, and floods. They've never seen
anything like this one.
And they'll say that next time.

Bill Yake

TOUCHSTONES
—March and Rally, Olympia, February 15, 2003

Our capitol is carved of local stone. Empty, Roman, symmetrical,
splinted this year against earthquakes and gravity—
it looms over the memorials of four wars.
Two gulls kite and veer. Beyond the fixed dome,
a swirl of shredding clouds half- hides
the transitory sun. Wind riffs; rain spits.
With voices and bodies faithful to the shapes of living beasts, we
have set breath and shoulders in motion: a serpentine procession,
      salamander-like, with incantations, weeping puppets,
      drums, a dirge, a dance, a murmuring dragon.

Summoning the memory of Viet Nam, a medic says it best,
"War is hell because it turns every inclination—even the intent
to heal - into destruction and into death."

Imagine the potential for salvage then. Native ferns reclaimed
from the bulldozer.
      Nootka roses and salal replanted.
      Or this capitol in monuments: its arches,
      columns, statues—a potential quarry in reverse.
Sculptors might discover owls perched here in alabaster; urge
mergansers skyward from
      this argillite, stroke loons as they chase free of marble and
      read the Braille ripple
      of ermines' sandstone vertebrae.
The other side of ruin.
These monuments that wars have made from still and stilling life.
      Coaxed back, freed, instilled with an elemental quickness.

The circle will. The circle must.

s place on this pole a chance
life, the ability to move.
at Beauty bush
  the corner of the house
comes what it's called
ly after we look and say *Yes*.

TEN YEARS OF POEMS: AN AFTERWORD

It is 20 degrees outside by the Poetry Pole this morning. Yakima is cold and dry. Not enough snow in the mountains to fill the reservoirs. Yakima Valley is an irrigated desert. Two more poems came in the mail on Saturday.

I have just come in from reading and photographing the poems that have been on the Poetry Pole since winter solstice. These poems, in addition to their time in the long, dark nights, have been in both rain and snow. They are the poems participating in a personal ritual, celebrating and honoring the poems, and the poets, who have used the Poetry Pole as a true source of poetry during the past ten years.

The Poetry Pole is in the garden at Blue Begonia Press. The Pole, intersecting the Path of Butterflies and Hummingbirds with the Path of the Mailman, validates and confirms the actions, and ways of being, of poetry in the world.

This is the 25th year of publishing poetry at Blue Begonia Press.

The Poetry Pole is egalitarian in its nature. It is not regional. Placed on Bell Avenue, it can be accessed by anyone from the street, and anyone by mail. The word POETRY is carved on both the East and West sides. Pins have been left on the Pole for poets to leave their work. An unseen sculpture, placed at its base by Marty Lovins, commemorates it.

I am the Keeper of the Pole. The Pole arrived as a vision. The title was given to me by Kevin Miller. It is a position I honor. I build the Pole with poems on a weekly basis, adding poems that arrive in the mail to those placed there by passersby. Some of the adventures of the Pole are known. After time in the weather, poems are put in a place of safe keeping.

The Pole is energy, She Who Shines For All, from nine kinds of flower, the single poetic theme of life and death, the question of what survives after the beloved.

The Poetry Pole explains itself. Children understand it.

Ten years ago I sent out a letter to poets telling them of the Poetry Pole.

This morning I gathered the more than 3000 poems that have been put on the Pole and collected, and had a symbolic moment, placing all of the poems at the base of the Pole and photographing them. I hope it honors the poets, some, Barry Grimes, Kevin Miller, Judith Skillman, Zev Shanken, Terry Martin, and Dan Peters, who have been significant contributors to the Pole. Some poems have been lost in wind and weather.

•

It's snowing again. I've just taken one last look at the photos I took of the Poetry Pole last week. Karen says, "Why do you keep taking those photos? Aren't they the same pictures over and over?" "No they're not. These photos are new like the poems. The good photographers go back to the same place again and again." I resist taking the camera as I go out to bring the poems into the house. The poems are beautiful. It's snowing hard. Let's see what they have to say.

•

There are 22 poems on the Pole. Barry Grimes pins "After the Flood" to the Pole on December 30th. He comes in the house afterwards and we drink a pot of Large Leafed Pu-Er Aged China Green. A Yunnan tea aged three years in bamboo casks in caves. Barry talks about consciousness, and the lack of it in the world. The word he uses is flood. He eschews the grander words and explanation. What he sees:

A long-legged teenage
blond farm kid
in old Levis and T shirt
yellow and white
feed company ballcap
squats on his heels
at the edge of the the river
....
says to no one in particular,
I saw it all last night.
Man said more than once,
Aint nobody lost.

The last to arrive in the mail is from Ann Spiers on Vashon Island.
"On the Gulf of Tonkin Between Wars, 2004. The title points to
Spiers's steady witness, "…and we float/in that moment when no
port awaits us, /no land owns us, no aircraft strafes us/and our
names are on no list to live or die." Her poem, "White Train," was
letterpressed and printed as an award-winning broadside more
than 20 years ago, and still witnesses on a wall in our house.

Barry's and Ann's work, the way they write and live—shows me
how poetry works in the world. Their experience is my
experience.

Judith Skillman sends four poems in the mail. She is careful to
distinguish which poems have been in other publications. She
has poems about the Pole. She recognizes and honors the Pole as
a true thing. In "Family Goat," Skillman writes, "We like to love
him despite the smell/ of his goatishness. On good days/ he
stands on top of the makeshift house/ and roars." The Poetry
Pole, like the family goat, has good and bad days.

"I Will Eat the Laws," is the title of Manuh Santos's poem, hand
written, and photocopied. Manuh, 24, a Mixteco Indian, began
college this week. "I will eat the laws because I am a/ free man.

The laws are raining/ like the rain from the vivid blue/ clear sky. The laws are falling slowly./ Choose them." Manuh graduated from high school in June. When he arrived here, at 17, he had never been to school. He spoke only Mixteco. He has learned Spanish and English with us. "I am going to eat the politician's/ laws because it was given by them./ I can eat them because I was born/ naturally inside my mother's stomach." Manuh's voice inspires the Valley. He teaches us many things. We have taught him to save his poems, and keep the originals.

Greg Freed is my friend. His new poems are "Named," about baseball, and "Rally" about ravens. "I hear what they are saying/ but I don't know what they mean." I got to know Greg through poems. The first poem he put on the Pole was "Hitler's Car." Greg and his wife, Suzie, just returned from spending a year at Holden Village, an ecumenical Lutheran Retreat Center above Lake Chelan. Greg was an emergency room physician for more than twenty years. He makes furniture. His writing goes back and forth between poetry and novels.

"I am painting angels," Keely Murphy writes. I have never met her, never seen her. She has four poems on the Pole right now: "Angels," "On Country Roads," "New Year," and "Of Shallow Water." When I sort through the poems from the past year, I suspect Keely will have put more poems on the Pole than anyone. Her poems always interest me. Exploring shallow water, she writes, "After nearly drowning in a pool in Oregon/ at the age of four, wearing a yellow bikini/ where my mom jumped in and saved me/ wearing a pink and white striped sweater and jeans/I found myself again....I will never drown, now./No matter how slick the walls, or how deep the steps/....even mornings when I wake up at sea." She finishes "On Country Roads":

> And it is always near, and it is always near.
> It is always near.
> On summer nights when the light blue gnats look holy

against the sunsets, glowing and soft and small.
While we come in, our hair smelling cold and like grass
And we were carried on, full of God.

Keely found the Pole through Dan Peters. She was attending
Yakima Valley Community College. Peters was her teacher. It is
Dan Peters, the poet, who stands back in awe, at the voice and
energy in Keely's poems. Keely Murphy has produced a
significant body of work during the last year. How much more is
there? What hasn't been put on the Pole? What is still coming forth?

Two other poems, "Breathing in Wartime," and "Body Count" by
Wenatchee poet Derek Sheffield, witness to our country's
appetite for oil and war, "…flaring/ spikes of a silent explosion."

> If I could only breathe
> more quietly, still that bloody racket
> circling beneath my skin,
> making zero after zero after zero.

My wife, Karen, and I have known each other for 40 years. We've
been married 36 years. On January 2, 2005, Karen turned 60.
My birthday poem for her goes on the Pole with the others.
Karen brings the integrity of every day into this house.
Nurturing the life around her, she says, "I am ready for what the
day brings me."

These are the poems before me this morning. These are the
poems at the beginning of a new time.

•

Poetry is service work. But it is not service work in the same
sense that one serves the community that one lives in. One
serves poetry, not the community. It is a vocation. Vocal. Calling.
Call and response. Being called to poetry, it seems to me, is being
called to listen. It is listening to the deepest sounds. Inside the

body. Inside one's self. To the quietest impulse. In the many ways of listening. In the way I am called, or you are called, to listen. This is the vocation as I understand it.

It is devotional work. And turning to it, one turns one's entire being, and in turn, one's entire consciousness changes everything that a life once was. A devotional act leads to a devotional process. It does not mean that one turns one's back to the world, but it does alter one's relationship to the world. And the world includes a person's family, including children. Including friends. Including jobs, or how money is made to pay the way.

Including those one does not know.

The gift exchange is about something else. It also requires a calling. A hearing. It is asking something from those who make contact. The act of picking up this book is a response to the call. You are being called. The act of putting a poem on the Poetry Pole is both call and response.

In this book, Blue Begonia Press presents our best, giving you our all-or-nothing, our acts of devotional work that reveal the work of poets who have shared their vocational work with us. We are the go-betweens, the *correveidiles*, of listening and telling. We are all part of the conversation.

Poetry takes place in unexpected places. It has to be this way. If poetry's value could be bought, it wouldn't be the democratic muse that it is. If poetry could be controlled, we know who would be in control. The raising of the Poetry Pole has consequences for the one who raises it. There are consequences for one who puts a poem on the Pole. And consequences for those who stop to read the poems. I can't tell you what they are.

I believe listening is making love. I believe listening is the deepest penetration. Listening is a political act.

Poetry brings the news of the other world. This world can be accessed. The principles are basic: extreme sobriety, practicality, and courage. In this tradition, like other mystical spiritual traditions, truth must be verified by the listener.

If something you hear, something you read, doesn't ring true from your experience, then it isn't true. The invitation is an entry point. The Poetry Pole is in our garden. It is part of our home, and part of our home-making. Karen and I are the caretakers.

I have always considered the Pole to be as important as any work I do, in addition to my roles in this house and this family. Beginning a new part of my journey this fall, Karen and I were returning from a visit with my friend Lynda Mapes, whose work as a reporter for *The Seattle Times* has brought her into our lives because of her interest in and reporting on Mexican families emigrating from rural areas in Michoacán into the Yakima Valley. Rob and Jackie Prout were with us. Mapes asked about the Pole, and over breakfast on the morning we left, we explored some of the living energy inside the archetypes of the Pole. Zack Krieger, Lynda's husband, likened the Pole to Chinese Posters. Barry Grimes and I have connected the Pole to Han Shan and Cold Mountain from the beginning. Cold Mountain, carving his poems on rocks, sticking them in trees. My primary image is the wooden lath fence surrounding Pablo Neruda's house at Isla Negra, in Chile. The Poetry Pole is the democratic newspaper of urban telephone poles. It is the spirit of broadsides.

Other images that came up that morning were Newspaper Rock, Burma Shave, Blank Book and Anazazi ruins. Someone said, "It is the intimacy and democracy of the refrigerator door." The weeping camel in the Gobi Desert.

Of course I embrace all of these. I love them all.

Driving off Vashon Island, Rob wrote all of these images into my journal. What his images do for this book is only part of what his friendship gives me.

These details show that there is nothing new, nothing novel, about the Poetry Pole. It represents ancient practice, and long apprenticeship.

Less consciously, but directly connected, is the debt that is owed to Robert Graves and his seminal book, *The White Goddess*. The spirit of Graves is everywhere. In my book, *This House*, I wrote this homage to Neruda, in a section called "The Poetry Pole in the Garden":

> Fence poles surrounding Neruda's house
> at Isla Negra become a memorial
> in their poverty, in offering themselves
> to each other, as an outpost far from the seats
> of power, in the manner in which they have withstood
> the terrorism of Pinochet and Nixon.
> They have become notebooks for those
> who would travel so far to see grand waves
> knocking against rocks found in famous poems,
> and collected surreal images of the well-traveled poet,
> for in looking up, before entering the grounds,
> one notices the letters, left like flowers,
> pressed into windswept wooden poles,
> sentries. Witnesses. Often, in our grieving,
> thinking we must act, that we're procrastinating,
> we don't see our grief work as making way.
> I weep before the fence poles at Isla Negra,
> puzzled and affirmed by the effortless *Fuck you*
> to power brokers, the soft manner
> in which the seeming dull pencil penetrates wood,
> leaving lasting impressions.

As an idea, the Poetry Pole exists as an antidote to the Poetry Business.

Judy Skillman drove over the mountains to read at the Pole. Derek Sheffield and Catherine Coan risked icy roads in winter to celebrate their work and put poems on the Pole. I never know what hours Dan Peters visits the Pole, but I know it's both real early and real late. Lynn Martin created her own Pole. And Derek Sheffield drew inspiration in creating other avenues for poets to publish their work. The Pacific Northwest Writers Association invited me to their conference and placed a pole at a central intersection of their writing sessions where writers pinned their poems.

Dan Peters' response, and work with the Pole, can only be understood as part of his total response to poetry, and to its call. His personal story requires its own essay, and can be found in the Preface to this book. Dan was the first person to pin an entire manuscript on the Pole. This single act redefined the Pole. On the summer morning I found the manuscript pinned to the pole, I sat on the lawn and read it, page by amazing page. When I finished, I took it into Karen, whose spirit does not call her to read the poems. I said, "Read this." She didn't put it down until she finished. We both said, as we never had, "This needs to be a Blue Begonia book." I went back out and sat on the lawn. Poet and journalist Ed Stover was out on his morning run, and I called him over. "Ed, look at these poems that were on the Pole." I left him to read. He knocked on the door when finished, and said, "If you need any money to publish this, let me know."

During the past two years, Dan has brought many Yakima poets along in their writing, and many of their poems have found their way to the Pole. Dan also brought Jenifer Lawrence to the poetry pole. She has given the heart of her emerging manuscript, here, in the weather, crafted poem by crafted poem.

My friend Terry Martin, who regularly puts poems on the Pole, reminded me of my own role—important and limited—as keeper of the Pole, during this past year. I emailed her some things that I liked about some recent poems. She thanked me, and then, firmly said, "But Jim, I never expect feedback from any of my poems that go on the Pole."

Each of these poems has been in weather. Each poet who has put a poem on the Pole has had a hearing far better than any editor, teacher, friend, or lover could give. Each poet has trusted a process larger than anything that can be explained. And each poem and poet has blessed my life. May the poems have more adventures, as William Stafford delighted in saying. May they also find new homes.

Jim Bodeen
January, 2005

Poetry Pole
225 So. 15th
Yakima, WA

Notes on Contributors

Every effort has been made to locate authors and make proper acknowledgment for all the work included in *Weathered Pages: The Poetry Pole*. In some cases, poets or publishers could not be located by press time. Blue Begonia Press would be grateful for any additional contact information so that proper acknowledgment may be made in future printings of this book.

A. K.: The poem "Women Gather" was put on the Poetry Pole with only her initials. Nothing more is known. The poem comes first in *Weathered Pages*. The editors think it sets the tone for this book.

John Akins: "My collection of war poems has helped me make something good out of something bad. The march to Khe Sanh in 1968 was an arduous, shocking experience that really tested my faith and resolve. The poem "On the Way to Khe Sanh" talks about how I found some respite, some peace. The poem "Going Back to Ky An with Cole" talks about my search for my soul and having my son be a part of it."

Carmela Alexander lives and writes on a small island in the San Juans. "'Agnes and Pat' honors aging, death, and courageous transition from duo to solo."

Jody Aliesan: "I took my own advice and left the country. I'll let the poems speak for themselves."

Linda Andrews lives in Walla Walla, WA and teaches at the community college. "In 'Downwind,' the sacrifice of body and home equals a down payment on the investment of a lifetime. Love's combination of responsibility and passion gives hope for warmth from materiality and the body."

Elizabeth Austen's author interviews and recordings of Seattle-area poetry readings can be heard every Monday on "The Beat" on KUOW, 94.9, public radio. Her poems have been nominated for a Pushcart Prize, and have appeared in journals including *The Bellingham Review, The Seattle Review, Switched-on Gutenberg*, and the anthologies *Poets Against the War* and *Pontoon*.

E.B. wrote this poem while in Juvenile Detention. It was placed on the Poetry Pole by her instructor, Tom Moore.

Dick Bakken: *"My most recent book is* Dick Bakken: Greatest Hits *(Pudding House Publications, 2005). These short poems are six of a hundred I wrote in my mid-to late-twenties while living in Portland, Oregon, 1966-1975, that paired with monoprints by artist Isabee Thiebaut make up our unpublished book,* Pinch Ass.

Molly Bales is a traveler and a dreamer who enjoys the changes that come with the seasons of a journey. "A great teacher once introduced me to the concept of reaching for the tip of the iceberg. This poem reflects a time when I tried to do just that."

Julie Barker: "Although I dreaded writing assignments as a student, it is now my favorite solo activity. I wish inspiration would strike more often. The everyday task of laundry folding sent me running to the computer. If cause and effect could be proven, I'd like to see to see what kind of poetry dusting or mopping might produce."

Lee Bassett gave up writing because it took up too much of his time. These are the last published poems of Lee Bassett.

James Bertolino has work published or forthcoming in *Ploughshares, Poetry, Notre Dame Review, Beloit Poetry Journal, Prairie Schooner,* and *Spoon River Review.* Nine volumes of his poetry have been published, and his work has been internationally anthologized. He has taught at Western Washington University and currently is Writer in Residence and Hallie Brown Ford Chair of Creative Writing at Willamette University in Salem, Oregon. "The poem 'Let Nature' was written while I was on the faculty of the University of Cincinnati, about 1980."

Jim Bodeen is the keeper of the Poetry Pole in the garden at Blue Begonia Press. He has been married to Karen Bodeen for 37 years. He has two black labs, Lacy Dreamwalker and Sister Sadie Sadie.

Karen Bodeen: "I am a banker, mother, and wife of a poet. I'm not a person of many words. I sew."

Linda Clein Brown: "'Chicken Fricassee' is one of a series of poems that examine the relationships between mothers and daughters and how much wiser we become. The Poetry Pole is like one of those pins we secure to maps that tell us where we have been or where we plan to go. We measure from that site and know we still have far to travel or we delight in how far we have come. Poetry is that map; the pole is that center."

Lindsay Brown lives on Bainbridge Island. She makes coffee for a living. She thinks about Yakima almost always. She is still looking for solid ground.

Bonnie Buckley: "This poem came about at a time when my life was filled with people of depth and a reasonable work schedule, and when I was living in a magical house built in 1829 in Cambridge, MA. The house was described as The Queen of the Neighborhood, and children passing by said they heard the voices of angels emanating from it. What they heard was one of the owners, a teacher of mine from the Longy School of Music, giving a vocal lesson. Nevertheless, while living in this house, there was very often great food, true friendships, much music, and a tremendous gathering of spiritual energy."

Anne Byerrum: "I have been a visual artist and or art teacher for my entire life. I started writing poetry ten years ago. This poem was a response to my cousin's death. My mother's twin sister and her children lived across the street from us for our first twelve years, so we all grew up like brothers and sisters rather than cousins."

Sev Byerrum: "I earn a living as an educator and I spend what I've earned as a photographer. This poem is about pre-dawn sounds early one winter morning."

Sharon Carter obtained her medical degree from Cambridge University. She is co-editor of *Literary Salt* (www.literarysalt.com), received a Hedgebrook residency in 2001, and was a Jack Straw writer in 2003. "'Ghazal for the Underdog' celebrates acceptance and non-violence while understanding the inevitability of death—the final equalizer."

Andy Clausen: Born in Belgium in 1943, Clausen was brought by his mother to live in Oakland, California at the age of 2. His chief books have been: *The Iron Curtain of Love* (Long Shot, 1985), *Without Doubt* (Zeitgeist, 1991), and his selected verse of 30 years, *40th Century Man* (Autonomedia, 1997). Of Clausen's poetry, Allen Ginsberg wrote: "The expensive bullshit of Government TV poetics suffers diminution of credibility placed side by side with Mr. Clausen's direct information and sad raw insight."

Linda Clifton, a sHADOWmARK, just completed a chapbook of her art and poetry, *Painting the Face of G-d*.

Cathy Coan: "I write, teach, and live in Manhattan Beach, California. This poem is about the joy of capturing the small things, and about the joy of being captured (not shared, perhaps, by the small things)."

Sky Cosby: "I make my home in the South Sound where I am hard at work raising a family, running Last Word Books and becoming a shellfish farmer. 'My Father's Socks' is a piece designed to summon up a picture of my pops, even for those who have never met him, and to soothe the pain of distance our separation elicits within me. 'When All Across My Skies' is sort of a silly, sing-song poem about my life and the state of the world at the time. It was written in spring, 2003. Sometimes I like to let rhyme and meaning blend each other out inside a work."

Michael Daley: "'Playing Catch,'" was written before and during the aftermath of 9/11 while I lived in Hungary and daily watched jets prepare for Afghanistan. 'Pariah's Tale' was written on the Anacortes to B.C. ferry in the silence of a crowd. I teach English at Mt. Vernon High School, Mt. Vernon, Washington.

Madeline DeFrees will be teaching in the Mountain Writers Pacific low-residency MFA program. "'The Paradise Tree' is a sonnet that was fun to write because the octave, in particular, makes use of unconventional rhymes. Alert readers will discover that it owes something to James Wright's 'A Fit Against the Country.'"

Jeni Nelson Delaney: "No extra words—let the poem stand on its own."

Rodolfo de León lives in Yakima, Washington with his wife and five children. "The poem, 'Things They Have Here to Take You Away from Here' focuses on the ravages of the Vietnam War from the perspective of the American soldier and the NVA soldier, and how reflections of life and death, individual and family and the aftermath of war, vis-a-vis the triptych, color the reality of the past and the present and ultimately, the future."

Alice Derry: Louisiana State University published Alice Derry's most recent collection *Strangers to Their Courage*. "Interestingly, both poems I chose for the Poetry Pole are about the war in Vietnam, the event which shaped my young womanhood. When that nightmare closed and all of us began the long process of healing, I thought I had done the war work for my lifetime. I was sadly much mistaken."

Brett Dillahunt teaches and writes in rural central Washington. "'Wasps' and 'Amoxiumpqua' are about family, blood, history, and empire in northern New Mexico."

Carolyn Calhoon-Dillahunt lives in Zillah, WA with her husband, Brett, her horses, and her cats. She teaches English and public speaking at Yakima Valley Community College. "In June 2000, we moved into our house on a couple of acres in Zillah, with plenty of lawn, landscaping, and animals to take care of. The street we live on has the same name as my oldest horse— Centennial. It's been home for five years."

Pamela Moore Dionne is the founder and managing editor of *Literary Salt*. Her work is found in print and online journals. Dionne has been a Jack Straw Writer and a poet in residence at Centrum, and has received a Jack Straw AAP Grant and an Artist Trust GAP Grant. "About 'The Democratic Way': In 1999 Clinton got caught doing one of many stupid things that gave rise to a media and Republican circus. I will never understand how America gets so caught up in these ridiculous scandals while completely ignoring the real disasters happening in the world around them. My frustration is what gave birth to this poem."

Jon Fischer is a graduate of Eastern Washington University's MFA Program and is currently living and teaching in Spokane. "A Chapel Undone" comes from his time as an undergrad in Seattle. It is his attempt to answer the challenge of using two words from a more or less random list in each line of a poem.

Joan Fiset: "Since 1995 I have worked with Vietnam veterans as a PTSD counselor at the Seattle Vet Center and in recent years in my private practice through VA Fee Services. 'Taxi' happened years before I began working with Vietnam vets. 'Ambush' is informed by what I've learned in the years that followed."

Jonathan Fletcher: "The poem was written as an answer to some memories. It took a little work on my part, and a little guidance from my good friend, Dan. I try to keep in mind that mistakes are just disagreeable opportunities."

Carole Folsom-Hill: "I love that writing poetry reveals my truths and allows others to discover their own truths. 'Rules' is a bold act of rebellion discovered in writing group. 'This Place' is La Casa Hogar, where family and home are created, and my spirit is nourished."

Greg Freed is a retired emergency physician who writes fiction and poetry and makes furniture. "Hitler's Car" is an account of an actual occurrence in his life, "Night Shift" was written in real time during his last night shift as an E.R. physician, and "Pessimist" is one of his many poems of self-disclosure.

Claire Freund graduated from Eisenhower High School in 2004 and is currently completing a one-year Rotary Youth Exchange in Vervins, France. She will attend the University of Idaho this fall.

Hilary Freund is a sophomore at Eisenhower High School. A distance runner, and a 2005-06 cheerleader, she remains close to her cat, Tubby. **Editors' Note:** Claire and Hilary Freund were in elementary school when they put their first poems on the Poetry Pole. They needed no instructions on what to do. The family still lives up the street.

Jeremy Gaulke lives with his wife and two cats in Yakima, Washington. "in the garden" was written in Walla Walla during the winter of 2003 for the poet's wife, Monica. She is responsible for posting it on the pole.

Jack Gilbert was born in Pittsburgh, Pennsylvania, in 1925. He was educated in Pittsburgh and San Francisco, where he later participated in Jack Spicer's famous "Poetry as Magic" Workshop at San Francisco State College in 1957. Soon after publishing his first book, *Views of Jeopardy*, in 1962, Gilbert received a Guggenheim Fellowship and subsequently moved abroad, living in England, Denmark, and Greece. During that time, he also toured fifteen countries as a lecturer on American Literature for the U.S. State Department. Nearly twenty years after completing *Views of Jeopardy*, he published his second book, *Monolithos*. The collection takes its title from Greek, meaning "single stone," and refers to the landscape where he lived on the island of Santorini. Gilbert is also the author of *The Great Fires: Poems 1982-1992*. *Monolithos* won of the Stanley Kunitz Prize and the American Poetry Review Prize, and *Views of Jeopardy* won the Yale Younger Poets Series. Both books were nominated for the Pulitzer Prize.

Barbara Smith Gilbert: "The concept of place (context) has held my internal attention throughout various external shape-shiftings. This poem followed the group planning of and participation in a Raymond Carver conference on the Yakima Valley Community College campus. With pre- and post-conversations, it included many wonderful reflections about Carver in Yakima and Yakima in Carver."

Richard Gold is the founder and executive director of Pongo Publishing, a therapeutic poetry program for homeless and incarcerated youth. He wrote "Sand" on a yoga retreat at the beach in the Yucatan, when his yoga teachers fell in love.

Barry Grimes has taught writing and literature in the public high schools for 33 years. "'ATF' from a dream. 'TCAATAM' is for Tom and the rest of us. 'ATHOAF' started one June day at Bodeen's."

Sam Hamill: "I'm Director of Poets Against War" and my selected poems and translations, *Almost Paradise*, was recently published by Shambhala. My translation of *Tao Te Ching* will be published this fall. About "The Nets"—anything I say about the poem detracts from the poem. Ciao."

Jim Hanlen is a chess master and teacher. He has a manuscript of creek poems and sometimes writes under that name. He is surrounded by the Chugach Mountains skyline in Anchorage, Alaska. Close by are excellent sites to pick up stones for garden walls. "No copyright infringement—they're in the public domain, free for the taking."

Sharon Hashimoto has taught literature and writing at Highline Community College since 1990. "'Interned…' originated from a wooden crate full of rocks that sat in my parents' basement for many years. I thought the image of the shadow-like pole was appropriate for the Poetry Pole."

Josh Henretig a Yakima native, now lives in the Seattle area with his wife and new daughter, Lillie. "The poem contributed represents the culmination of one feverish summer night in high school, in which rules were broken, love was contemplated, and the nuances of the world were discussed over coffee and haiku."

Kristin Henshaw, a 36-year transplant from Pennsylvania, teaches Japanese at Bainbridge High School and tries to balance family, friends, laundry piles, teaching, reading, working on poems, and messing around in her garden. "I wrote this poem for the grandmother who introduced me to *The Secret Garden*, nurtured my love of reading, taught me to use Latin names for plants, and celebrated her 100th birthday the day the magazine arrived in the mailbox. Part of the joy of spring is counting the daffodil buds each year and sending sprigs of heather in the mail to East coast family members still shoveling snow."

N. Kathleen "Kitty" Higgins: "One of these poems is about the final visit with a man I liked but did not know. As for the other poem, I am still seeking the philosopher's stone."

Abbey Howell: "I am 10 years old, almost 11. I attend school in Selah. My hobbies are softball, basketball, and dance. Sometimes I write poems with my Mom, Janelle. I like poetry because it does not have to rhyme. I write poetry because my Mom, Janelle, writes poetry. I look up to her. My poem, 'Friends,' was a song about my friends. My Mom, Janelle, asked me one day if it was a poem. I said to her 'it can be.'"

Janelle J. Howell lives in Selah, WA. She and her husband, Rod, have four children and three grandchildren. Janelle taught kindergarten in the Selah School District for nine years. She currently works behind the scenes, advocating family and community. "My poem, 'Moments,' was written for my Dad, Ted Jonas, during the period of his death. Unfortunately, I was unable to finish this poem until after my Dad passed away."

Tony Hunt is a writer and critic. He participated in the 1998 Stanford University Panel on Ethics & Aesthetics at the Turn of the Fiftieth Millennium following a reading of Gary Snyder's *Mountains and Rivers Without End*. His encounter with Barry Grimes at a National Endowment for the Humanities Conference on Shakespeare held in Ashland, Oregon in 1991 led to a series of exchanges between the two writers.

Paul Hunter: "I continue to dig into my past for clues about how we might behave. 'Washtub' is a common moment out of that rural world, making a virtue of necessity, savoring a family closeness (not merely enduring it) that is now unavailable to most Americans."

Connie Hutchison: "I write free verse and haiku, and have been active in the Washington Poets Association, Haiku Society of America, National League of American Pen Women (Seattle Branch President, 2004-06). At the Yakima library for a WPA reading (the first "road tour," about 1997), I talked with Jim, who told me about the Poetry Pole. We drove all around and never found it (!) so I mailed this poem, my tribute to William Stafford, the man and his generosity, his early morning writing practice, his use of 'plain' language to access deeper meanings. Weathering on the Poetry Pole until it becomes elemental, infusing water, earth and air, is the way poetry was for Stafford, like breathing. I am grateful to have this poem gathered, with those elements and spirit, in this anthology."

Cherryl Jensen is a poet and writer who lives in New Hampshire. She also leads creative writing workshops.

Chelsea Johnson is a student at Yakima Valley Community College.

Doug Johnson writes poems on scraps of paper between teaching at Davis High School and caring for his Angel and three kids. "Loopie's Hide" comes from a journaling project between Doug and Krystal reflecting on the childhood they shared together with juvenile Lupus. 40 poems were posted on the pole as a gift to Doug's family and the poetry community in Yakima. "Here it is in the common experience of life, unique and shared."

John Johnson: "I belong to the 4th generation of railroad workers, and lived in Yakima from 1946-1999. '13' was written in honor of all the readers at Davis High School Poetry Night, and in anger at all those who tried to get in their way."

Laurie A. Kanyer is a wife, mother, author, and servant working with pregnant and parenting women, many of whom have never known a day without loss. "This is my 9/11 poem. In September, 2001, I was a graduate student studying birth, death, and life transitions. I was also completing a manuscript on the subject of childhood grief. This poem emerged from the intimate knowledge I had of the reality of 9/11—children would be born never knowing their fathers and children would live with the tone of death. My book, *25 Things to Do When Grandpa Passes Away, Mom and Dad Get Divorced or the Dog Dies,* published in 2003 by Parenting Press in Seattle, offers 'coping activities' for grieving children, many hinted at in the poem."

Gayle Kaune recently moved to a garden overlooking Port Townsend Bay. Her book, *Still Life in the Physical World,* is available from Blue Begonia Press. "I originally wrote this poem as a part of some long forgotten exercise, but once it was written I knew it belonged on the Poetry Pole, in the middle of a lush garden, yet available to any adolescent girl walking by on 15th Street."

Tina Kelley is a Newark, New Jersey-based reporter for the *New York Times,* covering the environment, religion, and social issues. This poem, which was inspired by the woods of the northwest, appeared in *The Gospel of Galore,* her first book, which won a Washington State Book Award.

Cal Kinnear has been a teacher, bookseller, modern dancer, waiter, carpenter, grant writer, a developmental director for a social service non-profit and a private middle school—and a poet. "Three of the poems were born of a strong urge to bring the physical, outdoor world in to be chewed in the mouth of language; so it was a particular pleasure to see those poems go back outdoors to speak mutely from the Poetry Pole. The fourth poem was born of a cargo ship dreamt and the personless brutality of modern war."

Klipschutz (Kurt Lipschutz) lives in San Francisco and is the author of *Twilight of the Male Ego,* published by Tsunami Press in 2002. "'The Early Bird Catches the World' is the distillation of an early morning walk with Charles Potts and Jeff Jensen in September, 2002. It's all in the poem, hopefully!"

Zack Krieger: "My thoughts about war, suffering, and injustice were strongly influenced by my experience of being caught up in the war in Vietnam. I'm distressed that our country has become so imperial, xenophobic, and aggressive. I want to do what I can to resist this horror."

Dan Lamberton lives with his wife, Linda Andrews, in Walla Walla, WA, where he is a professor at Walla Walla College. "'All Winter' is about the joy one receives while watching the inner life of another person revealed through her hopes, actions, and faith."

Joy E. Langley "takes life too seriously. The Poetry Pole gave us a safe space in which to not be alone with our lamentations, original inspiration, hyper-distillation—and freedom to walk among giants. This pole—one plank in the boardwalk that would take me far away, and that has made all the difference."

Jenifer Lawrence: "I live in Poulsbo, Washington, near the Puget Sound. These poems are set in Alaska, where I spent my childhood. My sister was struck and killed by a car at the age of fourteen, after surviving a similar accident five years earlier. 'One Hundred Steps from Shore' is a child's recollection of events on the day of the second accident. 'The Feeding Tide' was written on my father's birthday, three years after his death. The task of baiting a salmon hook seemed endlessly complicated; today I can still see his hands, showing me how.

Marty Lovins is a jeweler and sculptor. He is one of the teachers. He makes shields.

Frank Malgesini grew up in Yakima and various parts of the Valley, and graduated from Selah High School, YVC and CWSU. He has lived in Mexico (Jalisco, Queretaro and Chihuahua) since 1974.

Lynn Martin, author of *Where the Yellow Field Widened: Elegies for a Lost Child* and *The Blue Bowl*, grows sunflowers, poems, fava beans, and hollyhocks in Gig Harbor, WA. "'Lace Curtains'—Grief moves the way light moves in and out of the clouds. 'Word'—Isn't every poet called to enflesh his answer to the world?"

Terry Martin is a 48-year old peri-menopausal English professor at Central Washington University and an avid hiker, reader, writer, movie-goer, dog-walker, river-watcher, and lover of the arts. Her work has appeared in over a hundred publications. "My poems are born in my journal, grow up and move to the Poetry Pole, and sometimes travel further from home, finding their way into literary magazines and anthologies."

Brooke Matson was born and raised in Yakima, but now lives in Spokane, WA. She only does three things: teaching, karate, and poetry. "Neglecting Your Easel" and "Elements" are from her more recent writing. The sestina "In the Valley" is a reflection and celebration of her home town, which she always returns to seasonally.

Rita Mazur: "I split my time between nine grandkids, five adult children, the Richland City Council, enjoying the Columbia and Yakima rivers, and writing. After months of struggling with iritis, an eye disease, I started preparing for limited or no vision. Every day I gathered memories of places, people, sizes, and shapes, and found joyous wonder in the process. The poem came to be after a visit with granddaughters, Kyle and Courtney."

David McCloskey, a long-time bioregionalist and poetry anthologist of Cascadia who recently retired from Seattle University, now lives in Eugene, Oregon, back in the old family house. "Perhaps poetry begins in conversation with the dead, and this 'letter' shows how a deeply rooted conversation continues before, through, and after us… Things have already changed since this letter, though we carry on…"

Kevin Miller lives in Tacoma, Washington. Blue Begonia Press published two collections of his poems: *Light That Whispers Morning* and *Everywhere Was Far*. "Pole poems are for street walkers and gardeners, for neighbors at first or last light."

James Milliron lives in the Wenas Valley with his wife, Gina, horses, dogs, cats and foster children, Zuley and Genny.

Susan Moon is a poet and teacher who lives near Prosser, Washington. "The poem 'Survival' was written during the time I was receiving chemotherapy for cancer. The affinity I felt for hardy survivors was intense that dry summer, the mottled shade from the locust's leaves an especially personal blessing."

Tom Moore: "I have been writing since I was in the sixth grade. At that time, three of us started our own publishing company. Now I teach English at Juvenile Detention. 'The Lost Road' was written just after the death of my father. We had just sold my parents' house and were making the last load of stuff from the house. My wife and I had been working all weekend long and were beat. While driving up Tieton Drive, I saw Jim and wrote the poem. He was the friendly face in a tough situation. 'She Became Her Mother' was written for my sister-in-law. I saw her at a family dinner and for a moment she looked like her dead mother. Her mother's death had hit us all really hard and I had promised to write a poem for Gayla. This was that poem. 'Lists' was on the inside of the funeral announcement for my father. He was a fighter pilot during WWII. He flew Hellcats. As a pilot, he knew the importance of order, therefore, he could write great lists."

Keely Murphy: "I live in the Yakima Valley, one block away from the Poetry Pole. It is in the center of the city. This is where everything begins. The Pole has arms."

German Nava graduated from Davis High School in Yakima, Washington.

Juan Ortega was one of the first abrecaminos at Davis High School in Yakima, WA. His long 12-part poem, "Acid Silence," based on Pablo Neruda's "Las Alturas de Machhu Picchu," was published in *With My Hands Full / Con Mis Manos Llenas* by Blue Begonia Press. Juan works for Quinta de Vista, Vision House, in Yakima, fitting eye glasses, and is still trying to figure it out.

Jorge Padilla "was raised on the streets. He knew people that smoked dope. He tried it once. He didn't like it. Well, he did get in fights for colors with homies, but he stopped. He don't do that no more. He was a cholo. He did gangbang. He used to be down for a color, but he doesn't want anybody to find out what it is."

Gail Pearlman is a community college English instructor, peace and justice activist, and Arctic backpacker. "'New Year's Promises' links images of our country's victims with the magnificence of a yet-untamed but gravely threatened wilderness. Written for my students, the poem expresses anger, grief, and a determination to keep speaking out."

José Pete: "My name is José Pete. I was originally born here, in Yakima, but most of my life was spent in Seattle. I was born here and lived here for four years, then we moved to Seattle until I was 13, and then my mom was in bad condition, so she wanted to pass away in Alaska, so I went with her. On May 9, 2003, she passed away. So then I came down to Yakima and finally met my Dad. I am 15 years old and I love cars. My goal in life is to be a car designer. The company I want to go under is Dodge or Chevrolet. I am Mexican and Native American and proud to be. I am José Pete."

Dan Peters: The poems I put on the pole were first published on the pole. The second poem, "Letter to Students Who Are Not Here" is in response to the deaths of three of my students from West Valley High School in Yakima. The students died after I had left to teach at Yakima Valley Community College. Two died while fighting fires and one while on a mission for his church. For a long time, I didn't have anything to say. Then I started looking at the hills around where I live. Barry Grimes, my high school teacher, is the friend who drove me around and talked about teaching, poetry and landscape.

Linda Pier grew up in Yakima, WA, where she taught high school English, French, and Spanish and shared her life for thirty-four years with her late husband, Tom Pier. Together, they raised one daughter, Leslie.

Tom Pier, born and raised in South Dakota, taught English at Yakima Valley Community College for thirty-three years. Blue Begonia Press published a posthumous collection of his poems, *Confluence*, in 2004.

Timothy Pilgrim: "I am a Pacific Northwest poet with over 60 poems in literary journals, but my day job is teaching journalism at Western Washington University. 'Hear No Evil' tells a hidden truth about America's war against Japan. My dad is dead now, but he loved this poem and its companion war poems at http://hope.journ.www.edu/tpilgrim."

Charles Potts has been publishing since 1963 and currently lives and writes in Walla Walla. The poems presented here evoke experiences from his youth in the 1940s and 1950s in Idaho.

Marjorie Power: "My most recent collection is *Birds on Discovery Island*, published by Main Street Rag Publishing Company early this year. My poem, 'To Tishku, Hovering' is one in a long series of poems in which I explored my own version of a female deity. I was well into the series when I wrote this poem."

Rob Prout: "I am a photographer and teacher. '1973' is a true story. It is a note written to a fellow teacher, Barry Grimes. We worked together to design a small autonomous school within our large high school. Our concept was rejected by the administration and the school board. My note to Barry is a memory of the thirty years of teaching between the two rejections."

Omar Ramírez Cruz is one of the *abrecaminos*, a graduate of Davis High School in Yakima, and a student at Central Washington University. His work was published in *With My Hands Full/Con Mis Manos Llenas*, by Blue Begonia Press. He wrote this poem for his high school graduation.

Bill Ransom: "I write poetry, short fiction, novels, and screenplays, and I teach writing at The Evergreen State College. After Somoza's overthrow in Nicaragua, people took to swimming on Sundays in what had been his private lake. During the Contra War, some Salvadorans and I took a break to drive up there. The contrast between the shell casings and the holiday drive told the larger story."

Jean Richardson resides in Portland where she regularly prostitutes her skill as a writer in various corporate venues. "Tomb Raider" was written for her niece, Beth Richardson, who was 15 at the time. Jean feels the sentiment applies to many niece/aunt relationships.

Ann Reierson: "I'm happy to be here in Yakima, raising my family. I still get night time anxiety and I had to sneak up on the Poetry Pole—I didn't want anyone to see me put up the poem. I am beginning to consider myself a poet."

Tim Reierson is an engineer on the daily adventure of raising three children with his wife, Ann. "Ordinary things help me understand the big truths in life. That's the voice of the poem."

Corey Robinson attended Yakima Valley Community College.

Judith Roche, poet, arts educator, editor, arts programmer, is the author of two poetry collections, *Myrrh/ My Life as a Screamer* and *Ghosts.* In 1999 she received an American Book Award for co-editing *First Fish First People: Salmon Tales of the North Pacific Rim.* She has taught poetry workshops and residencies extensively to adults, students, prisoners and others and is Literary Arts Director for One Reel, an arts events organization.

David Romtvedt: "I am a writer and musician from Buffalo, WY. The first time I ever had the chance to work as a poet was in the Washington Poets in the Schools Program. I worked at Davis High School in Yakima in the classrooms of Linda Brown, Jim Bodeen, Linda Pier and Jane Schwab. In my poems I make up people and places and plots but this poem came straight out of my daily life and reflects as well as I can what really happened."

Jillian Ross is an artist, writer, dancer who lives with her Blue Heeler— Chula Vista Linda Marie de la Mancha—in Wapato, WA. "'A Small Poem de Contrapunta' was written shortly after my return to the U.S. after an eight-year sojourn in Mexico. The poem seeks to define the mystery that exists when one slips between language, time, and culture."

Angel Ruiz is from La Huerta, Michoacán, and lives with his mother and father and little brother in Yakima. He likes video games and music. He enjoys basketball. Angel will be a junior at Davis High School in Yakima, Washington when this book is published. He is working in the fields this summer with his father. He wrote this poem when he was a freshman in high school.

Wendy Zárate S. graduated from Lengua Inglesa in Philosophy and Letters, and later taught at the Universidad, in Pennsylvania, and in North Carolina. She's in Minnesota now. She has published in *Graphite Processor*, *Metamorphosis* and *Literal Ink.*

Manuh Santos: "My name is Manuh Santos. I am from Oaxaca, Mexico. I am twenty-five years old. I live in Yakima, Washington, U.S.A. I graduated from Davis High School in 2004. Now I am attending Clark Community College in Vancouver, Washington. I speak three languages: Mixteco, Spanish, and English. I am a runner. I am part of the Clark College track and field team, and cross-country team. I want to be a history teacher. I like to listen to world music and read books about Greek and Roman history."

Jane Sarmiento Schwab: "As a teacher, I am inspired by Paolo Freire, who insists that educators teach the world and the word. 'Hop Fields, 1944' is a found poem from a friend who remembered his early days in Yakima. I am enchanted by childrens' desire for play, despite the circumstances."

Jo Shafer was a writing tutor at Yakima Valley Community College, a staff feature writer and copy editor for *The Central Washington Catholic*, and, before that, for *Yakima Herald-Republic* until illness forced early retirement. "Red Stove" first appeared in Shafer's fourth chapbook of poems, *Cutwork*, printed in 1997 and revised in 1999. "The piece is a conglomeration of bits and pieces from childhood memories, stories read and told, and a fascination with the Chinese concept of feng shui, in which the color red represents good fortune in life."

Zev Shanken: "For the past five years I have been lucky enough to have the chance to take a group of teenagers to Israel. I teach them from September to June through The Bergen County High School of Jewish Studies. I also teach Bible and Creative Writing at that school. The two other places I teach are Bergen Community College in New Jersey and Theodore Roosevelt High School in the Bronx, NY. It's fun to try similar lessons with all three groups: Jewish teenagers, college freshmen, inner-city Latino and African Americans. When people write poetry they don't look the way they look; poetry is a great equalizer."

Derek Sheffield: "I teach English at Wenatchee Valley College and have published a chapbook with Blue Begonia, *A Mouthpiece of Thumbs* (2000). These Pole poems come from the geographic valley of my home and the come from the political valley of our last four years. Each has surprised me and helped me, and one slipped in through the door of dream."

Harald Sigmar: 88 years old, Harald is one of the elders in the book. He and his wife, Ethel, recently celebrated their 65th wedding anniversary. "Ethel and I are very much alone these days, but it is with daily communication and life is very good. We are coming together in every way, sharing, reading and talking. She is my love that keeps me warm." Sigmar was ordained in the Lutheran Church in 1943, and served many different congregations. Always interested in writing as much as theology, it was often through the etymology of words that he found and pursued freedom. **Ed note:** Harald Sigmar began a conversation with Jim Bodeen in 1972 having do to with the relationship of theology and words. They spent two years revising and editing Sigmar's unpublished manuscript *Beyond Sanity*. The second half of the conversation, twenty years or so long, centered on poetry.

Karen Sigmar Mason and her husband, Richard Mason, will soon celebrate their 30th wedding anniversary. Karen teaches in the Issaquah School District. "I had a dream about making a quilt for my parents' 50th anniversary. We'd lived pieces of our lives in so many rich places, the occasion seemed to call for sewing it all together into a whole, colorful, complex piece—like their marriage. But alas, I had neither the skill nor the time. I realized our family works with words, the way some families work with art, so I gathered the images and penned them into a poem."

Bill Siverly is co-editor of *Windfall: A Journal of Poetry and Place*. His most recent book of poems is *The Turn* (2000), and he lives in Portland, Oregon. "'Confluence' is set at the confluence of the Snake and Clearwater Rivers where the towns of Lewiston, Idaho and Clarkston, Washington, are located. I was born in Lewiston, and this poem initiates a series of fifteen about growing up there; this series in turn constitutes the central section of a book of poems, a journey up the Columbia, Snake, and Clearwater Rivers called *Clearwater Way*."

Judith Skillman: "I have been writing poems since I was nine years old. The editors have been kind to me. These three poems were written in 2004, one in Cle Elum ("Magpie Eyes"), one in Bellevue ("Heat Lightning"), and one, inspired by marital counseling, in Kennydale, WA ("The Family Goat")."

Ann Spiers is a poet living on Vashon Island, immersed in so much green. "My poem: when I thought I was having a transcendent moment on a tourist foray off the Vietnam coast, I actually was descending into history. Not until I saw the Turner Joy docked at Bremerton did I know what the moment, the poem, really meant."

Clemens Starck is a retired carpenter and construction foreman living in western Oregon. "In classical Chinese poetry the account of searching for the Master in the mountains and finding him not there is repeated by various poets."

Erik Stevens, a transgendered man, lives and works at Holden Village, an ecumenical retreat center in the north central Cascade Mountains of Washington. He has many varied interests, from computing to art to hiking to writing. Erik has been writing poetry and essays since the early 80's, with most of his writings focusing on personal experiences and identity.

Ed Stover is a retired journalist who lives in Yakima, WA, and now spends his time writing and trying to keep up with his lovely wife's honey-do list. His poems, "Homecoming" and "The Face in the Window," are simply more attempts on his part to understand, through writing, his role in the world around him.

Joseph Stroud is the author of four books of poems. "My Lord What a Morning When the Stars Begin to Fall" is part of a series of six-line poems.

Loren Sundlee: "'Bucking' happens to grow out of personal experience as a farm kid in the midwest. Years later, I heard from others about the construction accident. To this day I'm leery of any machine more complicated than a pen."

Abril Talavera graduated from Lengua Inglesa, Universidad de Chihuahua, and taught in the University extension program.

Molly Tenenbaum's most recent book is *By A Thread.* "Mystery is crucial. I write a lot about the paradox between mystery and language being that which is supposed to clear up the mystery. It doesn't work, but it's a way to get closer to the mystery. My goal is articulation. I have things I want to say, things that are not sayable, and I don't even know how to say them."

Barbara L. Thomas, who recently moved from the Pacific Northwest to Kalispell, Montana, enjoys a scant acre of wildness—red fox, deer, hawks, meadowlarks, wildflowers. Her poem, "Wind Spirit," is a chant reminiscent of the voices of her mother's people, the Cherokee, while "Yellow Bell" celebrates the small pleasures of living close to nature.

Stephen Thomas: Following the reading for Charles Potts' 60th birthday celebration at Borders Books in Yakima, Thomas tore this poem out of his book, *Journeyman,* and put the poem on the pole under the streetlight. Thomas teaches at Cornish College of the Arts in Seattle.

Alexa Torres: "I especially enjoy writing short stories because I like to bring characters to life using vivid descriptions. The poem I wrote is about my Grandfather, whom I love very much. The poem describes how my Grandfather overcame his blindness and how he is still able to be a part of my life in a positive way."

Raul Torres: "I am Torito (little bull). Now I am a touchy-feely guy. This poem is my way of telling everyone, including my relatives, that I am not totally disabled because of my blindness. I feel at times that I am treated like an invalid because people do not realize that I can still do the majority of the things I used to do—and some things, even better."

Ann Tweedy: "I grew up in a small Massachusetts town and now live in western Washington, where I work for an Indian tribe. My poetry has been published in *Clackamas Literary Review, Rattle, Berkeley Poetry Review, Harrington Lesbian Fiction Quarterly*, and many other places. 'The Full Pulse of Happiness' is about the town I grew up in and a child's way of seeing. And it's about the forbidden and the mundane and escape."

Alma Varela–Uffenorde: "I have been a friend of the Bodeens for several years. The Poetry Pole is an image I carry of precious stories, told and untold. Our stories become one in the garden where The Pole stands."

Mary Ann Waters: These poems come from her book, *The Exact Place*, from Confluence Press. Mary Ann was a teacher. She participated in the conference "Teachers As Writers," hosted by Centrum. Several of her colleagues are in this book. Her two poems in *Weathered Pages* were put on the pole as a memorial after receiving news of her death after an illness.

Mary Whitechester: "'Death'" was written when I reached the age where beautiful and beloved older friends began to die. I was enraged to lose them. I lost my father since writing the poem and I thank him for giving me the world."

Amber Wherry: "I am now a fiber artist. Unfortunately, I no longer possess a copy of the poem I put on the Pole. I prefer to leave old work behind when it is finished, and head into a new challenge."

John Willson, whose chapbook, *The Son We Had*, was published as part of the Working Signs Series by Blue Begonia Press, lives on Bainbridge Island, Washington.

Vincent Wixon, from Ashland, Oregon, appreciated Blue Begonia and sHADOWmARKS. His new book of poems, *The Square Grove*, will be published by Traprock Books in 2005. "'Flood Town' was written in Portland during the Willamette's early spring flood of 1996. The events in the poem are based on speculation and hearsay."

Bill Yake: "At 58, my dreams are still vivid. Some of the images of sculpture come from an article I was reading about Tony Angell's artwork. Otherwise, I hope the poem speaks for itself."

ACKNOWLEDGMENTS & PERMISSIONS

Grateful acknowledgment to the magazines and books in which the following poems appeared and to the editors who selected them. Unless otherwise noted, copyright to the poems is held by the individual poets. The poems are reprinted with their permission.

Akins, John. "Going Back to Ky An with Cole" appeared in *On the Way to Khe Sanh*. John Akins Publishing, 2004. Reprinted by permission of the poet.

Akins, John. "On the Way to Khe Sanh" appeared in *On The Way to Khe Sanh*. John Akins Publishing, 2004. Reprinted by permission of the poet.

Aliesan, Jody. "please post" appeared in *Loving in Time of War*, Blue Begonia Press, 1999. Reprinted by permission of the poet.

Aliesan, Jody. "before you leave the country" appeared in *Seattle Lesbian Resource Center News*, 2002. Reprinted by permission of the poet.

Andrews, Linda. "Downwind" appeared in *Escape of the Birdwomen*, Blue Begonia Press, 1998. Reprinted by permission of the poet.

Bakken, Dick. "Ripe Cherries" appeared in *The Matrix: University of Washington Daily*. October 21, 1977. Reprinted by permission of the poet.

Bakken, Dick. "Priest of the Bees" appeared in *Poetry NOW,* 1981. Reprinted by permission of the poet.

Bakken, Dick. "Basho's Workshop" appeared in *Poetry Flash* #98. Reprinted by permission of the poet.

Bakken, Dick. "Blackfeet" appeared in *Abraxas*, 1968. Reprinted by permission of the poet.

Bakken, Dick. "Marge" appeared in *Yellow Silk: Journal of Erotic Arts*, 1985. Reprinted by permission of the poet.

Bakken, Dick. "Orchard" appeared in *St. Andrews Review* 1970-71. Reprinted by permission of the poet.

Clausen, Andy. "The Old Days" appeared in *Temple* 18, vol. 5 #2, published by Charles Potts. Reprinted with permission of the poet and Charles Potts.

Coan, Cathy. "Minnows" appeared in *Aviation,* Blue Begonia Press, 2000. Reprinted by permission of the poet.

DeFrees, Madeline. "The Paradise Tree" appeared in *Blue Dusk: New & Selected Poems, 1951-2001*. Port Townsend, WA: Copper Canyon Press, 2001. 184. Reprinted with the permission of the poet and Copper Canyon Press, P.O. Box 271, Port Townsend, WA 98368-0271.

Derry, Alice. "Reading the Names" appeared in *Strangers to Their Courage*, Louisiana State University Press, 2001. Reprinted by permission of the poet.

Derry, Alice. "We Were Both About Twenty" appeared in *Calyx*, Winter 2004. Reprinted by permission of the poet.

Dillahunt, Brett. "Wasps" appeared in *Spanish Crosses*, Blue Begonia Press, 2001. Reprinted by permission of the poet.

Dillahunt, Brett. "Amoxiumpqua" appeared in *Spanish Crosses*, Blue Begonia Press, 2001. Reprinted by permission of the poet.

Fischer, Jon. "A Chapel Undone" appeared in *The Seattle Review*, 2000. Reprinted by permission of the poet.

Fiset, Joan. "Ambush" appeared in *Raven Chronicles*, 2004. Reprinted by permission of the poet.

Fiset, Joan. "Taxi" appeared in *Big City Lit: Vietnam Issue*, 2001. Reprinted by permission of the poet.

Gaulke, Jeremy. "in the garden" appeared as a broadside from The Temple Bookstore. Reprinted by permission of the poet.

Gold, Richard "Sand" appeared in *Vox Populi: Seattle Poetry Festival Anthology*, 2000. Reprinted by permission of the poet.

Hashimoto, Sharon. "Interned in the Heart of the Country, My Grandfather Searches for Fossils" appeared in *Milkweed Chronicle* 1987 and also appears in *The Crane Wife*, Story Line Press, 2003. Reprinted by permission of the poet.

Hamill, Sam. "The Nets" appeared in *Almost Paradise: New and Selected Poems and Translations*, Shambhala Publications, 2005. Reprinted by permission of the poet.

Henshaw, Kistin. "In Late Winter" appeared in *Scotch Broom*, Winter 1995-96. Reprinted by permission of the poet.

Jensen, Cherryl. "You, Me, Her, & Us" appeared in *Northern New England Review*, 2001. Reprinted by permission of the poet.

Kelley, Tina. "Having Evolved from Trees" appeared in *Gospel of Galore*, Word Press. Reprinted by permission of the poet.

Lamberton, Dan. "All Winter" appeared in *Seasons of Faith*, Pacific Press. Reprinted by permission of the poet.

Martin, Lynn. "The Blue Bowl" appeared in *The Blue Bowl*, Blue Begonia Press, 2000. Reprinted by permission of the poet.

Matson, Brooke. "Neglecting Your Easel" appears in *Reflection: Gonzaga University Journal of Art & Literature*, Fall 2004. Reprinted by permission of the poet.

Moon, Susan. "Survival" appeared in *The Telling Signs*, Blue Begonia Press, 2000. Reprinted by permission of the poet.

Murphy, Keely. "Angels" appeared in *Prism*, 2005. Reprinted by permission of the poet.

Murphy, Keely. "Distilled" appeared in *Prism*, 2005. Reprinted by permission of the poet.

Pearlman, Gail. "New Year's Promises" appeared in *Two-Year College Association Pacific Northwest Newsletter*, Spring 2003. Reprinted by permission of the poet.

Pier, Linda. "The Sage of Home" appeared in *Confluence*, Blue Begonia Press, 2004. Reprinted by permission of the poet.

Pier, Tom. "Down to the Cottonwood Bottoms" appeared in *Confluence*, Blue Begonia Press, 2004. Reprinted by permission of the poet.

Pier, Tom. "The Man Who Fished Too Much" appeared in *Confluence*, Blue Begonia Press, 2004. Reprinted by permission of the poet.

Pier, Tom. "On the Way to Salpetriere" appeared in *Confluence*, Blue Begonia Press, 2004. Reprinted by permission of the poet.

Pilgrim, Timothy. "Hear No Evil" appeared in *Jeopardy Magazine* 2001. Reprinted by permission of the poet and by permission of editors of *Jeopardy Magazine*, Western Washington University Press.

Potts, Charles. "Hide" appeared in *Lost River Mountain*, Blue Begonia Press, 1999. Reprinted by permission of the poet.

Potts, Charles. "Harrowing" appeared in *Connections*, Keith Browning Publishing. Reprinted by permission of the poet.

Power, Marjorie. "To Tishku, Hovering" appeared in *Tishku, After She Created Men*, Lone Willow Press, 1996. Reprinted by permission of the poet.

Ransom, Bill. "Doble Traccíon" appeared on *War Baby* (compact disc), Wordman Production Co. Reprinted by permission of the poet.

Roche, Judith. "Hunger" appeared on *Subtext* website, 1998. Reprinted by permission of the poet.

Shafer, Jo. "Red Stove" appeared in *Cutwork*, Hattiejo Designs, 1997. Reprinted by permission of the poet.

Sheffield, Derek. "Breathing in Wartime" appeared in *Mirror Northwest*, 2005. Reprinted by permission of the poet.

Sheffield, Derek. "Firefighters Walk into Mountain Sports" appeared in *Poet Lore*, 2004. Reprinted by permission of the poet.

Skillman, Judith. "The Family Goat" is forthcoming in *Northwest Review*. Reprinted by permission of the poet.

Skillman, Judith. "Heat Lightning" appeared in *Field*, Spring 2005. Reprinted by permission of the poet.

Skillman, Judith. "Magpie Eyes" is forthcoming in *Illya's Honey*. Reprinted by permission of the poet.

Stroud, Joseph. "My Lord What a Morning When the Stars Begin to Fall" appeared in *Country of Light*, Copper Canyon Press. Reprinted by permission of the poet.

Thomas, Stephen. "Perspectival" appeared in *Journeyman*, Tsunami Press. Reprinted by permission of the poet and publisher.

Tweedy, Ann. "The Full Pulse of Happiness" appeared in *Swell*, New Town Writing, Summer 2005. Reprinted by permission of the poet.

Waters, Mary Ann. "On the Trail" and "Although It's Late In the Season" appeared in *The Exact Place*, a James Hepworth book from Confluence Press. Permission requested.

Wixon, Vince. "Flood Town" appeared in *Calapooya*, 1997. Reprinted by permission of the poet.

1. Write a poem on this page
2. Tear it out of the book
3. Pin it somewhere